School
Effectiveness

A Lucky Duck Book

School Effectiveness

Supporting Student Success Through Emotional Literacy

Marilyn Tew

P·C·P

Paul Chapman
Publishing

 Paul Chapman Publishing
A SAGE Publications Company
1 Oliver's Yard
55 City Road
London EC1Y 1SP

SAGE Publications Inc.
2455 Teller Road
Thousand Oaks, California 91320

SAGE Publications India Pvt Ltd
B1/I 1 Mohan Cooperative Industrial Area
Mathura Road, New Delhi 110 044
India

SAGE Publications Asia-Pacific Pte Ltd
33 Pekin Street #02-01
Far East Square
Singapore 048763

www.luckyduck.co.uk

Commissioning Editor: George Robinson
Editorial Team: Sarah Lynch
Designer: Nick Shearn

Library of Congress Control Number 2006904347

A catalogue record for this book is available from the British Library

ISBN 978-1-4129-1309-6

Printed on paper from sustainable resources
Printed in India at Replika Pvt Ltd

Contents

CD-ROM 1 Contents

Student Handbook (24 pages, see Section Seven)

Printable Resources (see Section Four)

CD-ROM 2 Contents

TalkiT LIght Edition (TalkiT-LE)

Trial version

Preface and Acknowledgements

The Story of this Book

The seeds of this book were sown about ten years ago when I was studying for my Masters in Education. I began the research by enquiring into the impact of PSHE lessons on students' self-esteem and self-efficacy. As those early forays into research progressed, I became increasingly interested, not just in the way the curriculum can effect change in students, but in what kind of change the students perceived to be necessary. I began to enquire into how students perceived life at school and how the school system and the adults who work in it could provide experiences that would be more facilitative of learning from a student's perspective.

The journey has been long and the way often rough and hard going. Therefore I have many people to thank for their enormous encouragement and for keeping me motivated when I might have given up. Firstly I must thank my amazing family who so steadfastly believe in me and the work that I am trying to do. Paul, David, Sheetala, Liz, Esther and Philip have variously read drafts, motivated me to keep going and been supportive when I plunged into despair. In addition to my family, Norma McKemey, Sandie Sargent, Tony Mann and Tim Bond have been faithful friends and sounding-boards, helping me to decipher a clearer path when the way became obscure.

The software that accompanies the book was designed by Steve Martin who has given selflessly of his time and talent to make TalkiT happen as has my friend and colleague Tony Mann. I cannot thank them enough. Then there are the schools who have allowed me to trial the ideas, giving me access to their technicians and students. Thank you to Gill Price, Connor McDermott, Sue Gray, Pam Stoate, Andy Griffith, John Griffith, Phil Cooke and Dave Sheppard. Last, but not least, my thanks go to the students who have given their feedback on various incarnations of the questionnaire and helped me to write the student materials. In particular, thank you to the year eight students of Mayfield Middle School on the Isle of Wight.

Section One

The Background

In this section you will consider:

- ► students' views of success in school
- ► the students' lifeworld
- ► domains and constructs.

- ► links with emotional literacy
- ► social and emotional aspects of learning

I have been in the world of education as student, teacher, middle manager, senior manager, lecturer, consultant and trainer for many years. It would not be hard for me to give a rationale for education, produce an essay on learning theory or create a policy for the implementation of some new educational initiative. In other words, I am conversant with the world of education from an adult point of view. Up until six or seven years ago, that was enough. I was content to be considered competent and knowledgeable by my colleagues and clients. Then I noticed in myself a growing disquiet that unsettled my professional equilibrium. It wasn't that I became less competent or had a crisis of confidence. Rather I found myself increasingly curious about how young people perceive their educational experience. Sometimes challenges to attitudes and perceptions creep up on us and we find it hard to track back through the labyrinth of thoughts and experiences to the source of the disturbance that precipitates a process of change.

Perhaps it was a home full of teenage children, who asked difficult questions, didn't accept conventional reasoning about school, and cast doubt on my accumulated educational wisdom. Perhaps it was the opportunity for professional reflection that came from studying for a Masters in Education. Whatever the triggers, the result was that I noticed a growing gap between my knowledge of adult perceptions of education and school and my awareness of students' perceptions. Not only did I have little comprehension of how students perceived their school experiences, I did not accord any real weight or importance to their view. In other words, I had a conception of education that was 'done to' a group of young people. The curriculum was a body of knowledge, understanding and skills that was 'covered' in a programme of study, translated into a scheme of work and 'delivered' in lessons. The unquestioned assumption that underlay this view of education was that students were passive recipients of knowledge.

As a teacher who trained in the '70s, I knew about the child-centred philosophy of education. I was aware of the work of Neil (1962), Dewey (1938), Rogers (1969) and Rousseau (1762). Later, I read Brandes and Ginnis (1986), Button (1971, 1982), and Stenhouse (1967, 1985). Of course I thought that students needed to be motivated, to work, to learn information, to engage with the concepts being presented and own their learning. However, I did not stop to consider their views on the learning process or what they thought enabled them to be efficacious. If I thought about it at all, I would have said that the most active agents in education were the policy makers, the curriculum designers, the curriculum managers, the lesson planners and so on. In other words, agency lay in the hands of the adults of the education system. The students were actively engaged in their own learning, but only as directed by the adult world. I don't think I ever stopped to think about what went on in the hearts and minds of the young people in front of me as I taught.

In my work as a trainer and consultant, I have not found my position to be unusual in educational circles and many teachers rarely consider a student's perspective unless it challenges their ability to 'deliver' a lesson. We enquire into a student's world only if emotions run high or behaviour is inappropriate to learning.

The situation is changing however. The process of change that I noted in myself is part of a changing agenda on a much wider scale. Starting towards the end of the 20th century and continuing on into the 21st, there has been a gradual shift in emphasis from an adult only view on what is good for a child to a recognition that young people also have a view and should have a voice. Students are no longer to be 'seen and not heard' as objects of legislation and provision, but given the opportunity to express their views on the issues that relate to them. In education, this shift has resulted in increasing numbers of school councils, student questionnaires to inform school change and a greater emphasis on learning from the perspective of the learner in OFSTED (Office for Standards in Education) inspections. In the wider arena of policy and government legislation, the changing emphasis is seen in The Children Act and the resulting national framework for change entitled 'Every Child Matters'.

While I am heartened by the move to give greater weight and credence to students' views on their education and learning, I find that it is but a single current in an educational river that is rigidly defined by nationally set criteria of success.

Three educational developments in the last 20 years seem to have created the framework within which the policy makers and the adult world define success in education. There are the:

- ▶ introduction of GCSEs
- ▶ advent of the National Curriculum
- ▶ formation of a school inspection body (OFSTED).

The combined effect of these three initiatives has resulted in school success being measured by academic achievement in terms of National Curriculum tests at the end of each key stage and in the number of students gaining five or more A*-C grades at GCSE. When success criteria are as prescriptive as these, the inevitable result is a narrowing of the curriculum, concentration on teaching for the test, and a focus on the acquisition of narrowing knowledge and curriculum skills in order to get the most students to or over the required National Curriculum level or GCSE grade.

As I thought about the narrowness of the political and official perspective on success and achievement, so my curiosity grew. I became increasingly interested in finding out what students see as important to doing well in school. This question became the focus of the research that led to my doctorate. It yielded a wealth of insights into the daily experience of students and the ways in which they see their life at school.

Students' views of success at school

My research asked the question, 'What do students think is important to doing well at school?' It involved getting inside the way young people think and creating a map of the way they construe life at school. In order to understand the research findings, we first have to think about how people make sense of their world.

The theoretical method I used was Kelly's Personal Construct Psychology. This is based on a premise that each of us has an internal personal map, which we use to find our way around the world we live in. We drew our map during childhood when we set about exploring the meanings in our physical and emotional environment. Kelly likened children to little scientists, who are constantly exploring, discovering, weighing one piece of information against another and testing out their latest hypotheses in new situations (Kelly 1955). They learn that some bits of metal are hot and to be avoided, such as radiators and irons, while other bits are cold and can be useful, such as spoons and tricycles. They constantly try things out, then retry them in a different situation and slowly piece together what works for them in their particular set of life circumstances. For most children, the voyage of discovery is monitored by loving parents or carers, who ensure that they come to no lasting harm as they carry out their personal experiments.

In the same way as children explore their physical world and put it into categories such as 'useful : useless', 'harmful : harmless', 'edible : inedible', 'tastes good : don't like' and so on, they also explore their emotional world. They create similar emotional maps to guide them in their meaning making or personal understanding of the 'way things work'. Hence some children learn that if they are persistent enough, they get what they want, while others learn that blind persistence only gets them into trouble. Similarly, others discover that a nice voice and an attempt at 'please' gets good results from parents, while others discover shouting and whining to be useful tactics, particularly when adults are tired and low on energy! These discoveries are made through a process of trial and error and result in the construction of personal maps which are used for navigating life experiences. The map or navigational aid is made from countless experiences of applying meaning to perceptions of the world around them. This personal meaning is called a 'construct' because it arises out of the way people construe or create understanding from what they experience.

Constructs are like two way streets because they involve two polar opposite ways of perceiving an experience. These constructs can be expressed as, 'Is … and is not …' For instance, I might say, 'This is fair and just and is not biased' or, 'This is kind and is not cruel.' Everyone has a different map because each of us has a unique developmental history. Even the same events impinge on people differently because their unique temperament, dispositions and perceptions cause them to construct a different 'take' on any given situation, event or experience.

I was recently dealing with an incident in school where a boy and a girl had witnessed a fellow student cutting herself. The boy said, 'Tanya was slitting her wrists. She's trying to commit suicide and you must do something to stop her. It's awful.' The girl said, 'Tanya just wants to be left alone. She doesn't want anyone to know that she is cutting her arms. She uses scissors and the cuts aren't deep, though they do bleed.' Here are two very different accounts of the same event. Tanya is cutting herself and from the boy's perspective, she is in danger of imminent death. He sees this as a crisis situation and his emotional response to the situation matched his sense of urgency. He was agitated, distressed, insistent and persistent. The girl, on the other hand, was much more matter of fact about the situation, she did not see it as life-threatening. She thought we should leave Tanya alone because that's what she wanted and that the cutting was not very bad. She thought that Tanya was sorting things out on her own and would be fine if she was given the time to work it through.

We could ask which perspective was 'true'? Which was the more accurate account of reality? We could look for truth by inquiring into the facts of the situation such as measuring the depth of the cuts, looking at their exact location on Tanya's arms and the quantity of blood she had lost. Or we could inquire into Tanya's mental health and emotional stability. Another way of exploring this situation is to delve deeper into the history of the observers. Here, we would find that they boy comes from an Afro-Caribbean heritage with close family ties and a tendency to take injury of any kind very seriously. He has already experienced an attempted suicide in his family and is distressed that history might repeat itself. The girl, on the other hand, comes from a family where dad left home when she was a toddler and mum has brought her up to be very self-reliant. She is used to fending for herself and making light of things that other people might consider very distressing.

The event illustrates that 'reality' is not a straightforward idea. It is very complex and individual perceptions are a product of interpretation depending on the temperament, social history, cultural history, intellectual understanding and social connectedness of the observer. In other words the boy and girl had socially constructed 'realities' which were different for each of them. You will probably have noticed these kinds of differences in your everyday work in school. For instance, siblings brought up in the same house, with the same parents, doing the same things and with similar experiences can have very different ways of responding to school. This is because they have construed life differently. The events of home, relationships and interactions alongside position in the family have had a unique impact on the disposition and temperament of the individual resulting in very different responses and reactions.

As we have seen, each person has a unique set of constructs; a very personal way of viewing the landscape of life. Yet, despite the enormous number of constructs and ways of construing, there are also similarities in the ways that people perceive and make sense of the world. In any work or faith setting, for example, it is likely that people will construe similarly in relation to the common cause. The very nature of being part of something causes them to assume a similar value system or to construe in a similar way. It is also true that people tend to find it easier to accept someone with similar constructs, or put another way, with a similar value system, than someone with a very different one. So we tend to get on with people who think like us and treat those who think very differently with a degree of suspicion and scepticism.

I was interested in finding out how students aged 11 to 14 construed life at school, particularly in relation to the ability to do well. In other words, I wanted to find out whether there was any similarity in the ways students made sense of their school experiences. I began with over 80 students in groups of five or six and used an adapted version of Kelly's Personal Construct Theory to elicit personal construing in relation to doing well at school. A personal construct was accepted if there was consensus in the small group that it mattered to doing well in school. This process led to agreed constructs such as 'believe in their own abilities' or 'in touch with what they feel'.

Once a construct was elicited and agreed, I asked the question, 'What would I see these people doing?' The group of students was asked to provide evidence of this construct in real life by imagining that they were watching people who had the qualities, attitudes, values or skills and give examples of the sort of things they might do.

One of the constructs was 'able to communicate well' so I asked questions such as, 'How would I know two people were communicating well?' or, 'If I was a fly on the wall watching two people were communicating well, what would I see them doing?' or 'If two people couldn't communicate well, what would they be doing?'

A richer picture was gained by using a technique called 'Day at the Zoo' (Mann, 1994). Young people were asked to think of a successful student as an animal or composite animal that represented the characteristics they thought led to success. The results included animals with small mouths and large ears for students that can listen not only to words but to feelings behind the words and don't talk or shout out in class. Others had sturdy legs so that they could stand up for themselves and not be easily pushed around. Again, once a construct was identified, the students were asked to describe the behaviours that would show the presence or absence of this construct.

These processes resulted in 154 agreed pieces of behaviour that were evidence of student's construing of life at school.

Next I sought to ensure that the behavioural evidence had meaning in the view of a different set of students. I wanted to know if other students, in a different context, could make sense of the 154 descriptions of behaviour and if their understanding would describe a framework for successful or effective life at school from a student's point of view. The constructs were written as statements on individual cards and presented to six pairs of 13 year old students who were asked to sort them into categories of behaviours that they thought belonged together. Once they had agreed which behaviours described the same thing, they gave the group of statements a title. A comparison of the groups of statements under each title across the six pairs of students led to a distilled framework of constructs. Not only did the students provide similar names for the constructs, there was remarkable consensus on which behaviours described which construct.

Gradually it became clear that there was considerable agreement among the students in terms of constructs both within a school and across schools. Once I had established that a common understanding of what makes a successful student existed in the minds of the young people, it seemed that this could be used as a way in to talk about the issues that they think matter to doing well at school.

Understanding the students' lifeworld

The most startling thing about the results of the inquiry into student constructs was that they made sense of their school world and of their ability to do well in school almost entirely in personal and social terms. They did not mention tests, exams, grades, levels or even school subjects. Their understanding of 'the way it is' in school was almost entirely construed in personal, social and emotional terms. They talked about personal qualities such as confidence, integrity, optimism, imagination, motivation and self control and then of social skills such as understanding and getting along with other people (Tew, 2002).

A German philosopher, Habermas, called this subjective understanding of 'the way it is round here' as the lifeworld (Outhwaite, 1994). The lifeworld describes the shared, unquestioned knowledge and practice that becomes the norm for functioning and relates mostly to the personal and moral spheres. Habermas also writes of another sphere which he calls the 'systems world'. In a school, this would describe the rules, routines, policies and regulations that circumscribe the way the school is organised.

This work has been further substantiated in the past year using a statistical analysis of 380 student responses to the behavioural statements.

From the students' point of view, the lifeworld is much more important to doing well at school than the systems world. In the domain of motivation, they acknowledge the need to conform to the systems world in keeping the school rules and sticking to the routines of classroom practice, but the real key to getting on well in school and being successful is governed by an understanding of the lifeworld.

Domains and constructs

In the three years since my doctorate in 2002, I have continued to work with young people in a number of schools to refine the framework of constructs. The results of these years of enquiry have identified five main areas of personal and social development that need to be addressed if a student is to do well in school. It might be helpful to think of life at school as a territory. Constructs represent the navigational aids that students use to find their way round the territory. The more skilled they are in each of the 12 constructs, the better they will be able to find ways of doing well or being successful at school. The students identified 12 constructs which are:

- ▶ optimism
- ▶ imagination
- ▶ integrity
- ▶ confidence
- ▶ empathy
- ▶ being helpful

- ▶ using anger well
- ▶ working together
- ▶ fitting in
- ▶ communicating well
- ▶ keeping going
- ▶ staying on track.

Each of the 12 constructs was described by a set of behaviours which have internal consistency as a separate and discreet set of ideas yet they are all related to one another as features on the bigger map of 'doing well at school'. When the students' constructs were compared to research literature from across the world, it became clear that the constructs formed clusters or groups that belong together. I have called the clusters 'domains' because they represent distinct regions on the 'doing well at school' map.

The five domains are:

- ▶ self-awareness
- ▶ self-control
- ▶ getting on with others
- ▶ understanding others
- ▶ motivation.

Goleman (1996, 1998) identified a framework of emotional competence that had five very similar broad areas of competence. His were personal competence comprising self-awareness, self-regulation and motivation and social competence comprising empathy and social skills.

The diagram shows the way in which the students clustered the 12 constructs into five domains. When teachers are able to understand the ways in which students construe successful life at school, they find new ways of relating to the learners in their classrooms. The concepts and skills found in the five domains and 12 constructs are the 'ways in' to creating meaningful connections with students. These are keys to unlocking student potential and facilitating a happy and fulfilled school life which in turn brings a whole range of successes, not only academic, but social, emotional and personal.

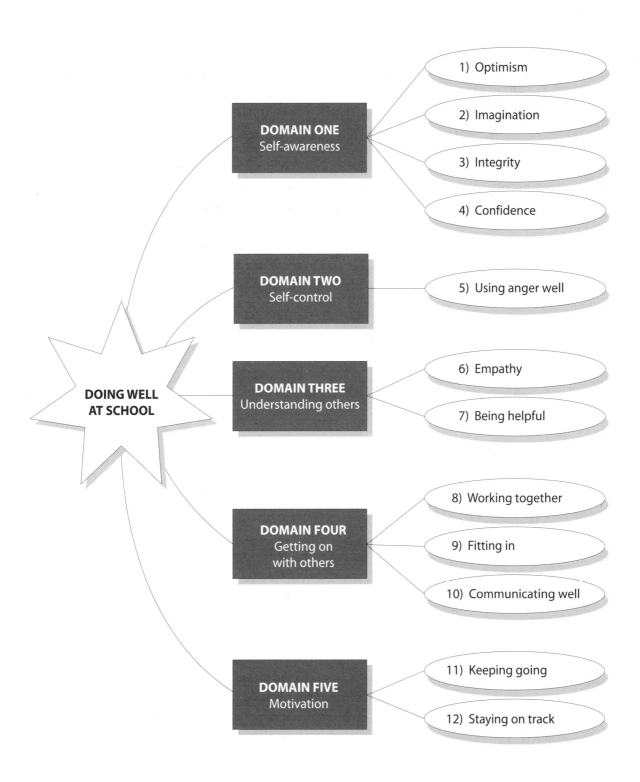

Links with emotional literacy

It seems appropriate at this point to draw together some of the links that the students' understanding of their school world have with emotional literacy. Until about ten years ago neither of the terms 'emotional literacy', or 'emotional intelligence' were heard very often. It is interesting to note though, that as far back as the 1920s Thorndike was writing about emotional intelligence (Thorndike, 1920). In the 1990s the work of many eminent psychologists came together to create a new stream of thought that is variously labelled emotional intelligence, emotional literacy and social, emotional competence. Then in the late 1990s, Daniel Goleman wrote his popular works on emotional intelligence that brought the ideas to more general public awareness (Goleman 1996, 1998).

In education, the ground-breaking work of Howard Gardner on multiple intelligences prepared the ground for a focus on the aspects of learning that have come to be called emotional literacy. Gardner (1983, 1991, 1993) included two personal intelligences in his nine types of intelligence. He proposed intrapersonal and interpersonal intelligences as a person's ability to access their own internal feeling states and their ability to relate to the outside world and function and in the wider community. Interpersonal intelligence includes the ability to notice, understand, make distinctions between, empathise with, relate to and work with other people. Intrapersonal intelligence involves the ability to be introspective, to notice, recognise, name, discriminate between and manage our own feelings, and then to draw on them as a means of understanding and guiding behaviour.

Nowadays, the terms emotional literacy, emotional intelligence and emotional competence seem to have the greatest popularity and are often used interchangeably. Few people bother to tease out the differences in meaning. I will attempt here to show the distinctions and the reader can decide which term they want to use on any occasion. Work in schools for the personal and social development of students deals with all three at some time or other.

> Emotional intelligence is a concept originally developed by two Americans called Salovey and Mayer. It is a measure of someone's ability to perceive and identify emotions, to use emotions to facilitate thought, to understand how emotions fit together and to manage emotions in self and others (Salovey and Mayer, 1990). Emotional intelligence is measured using clinical psychological testing and is an ability in the same way as we understand cognitive ability.
>
> Emotional literacy and emotional competence seem to be much more about an application of emotional intelligence. As Peter Sharp wrote, 'emotional literacy means using your emotions to help yourself and others' (Sharp 2001 p1). Sharp also says that, 'emotional literacy may be defined as the ability to recognise, understand, handle and appropriately express emotions.'

By this definition, there is little difference between emotional literacy and emotional intelligence except that the former seems to be more openly accessible than the latter. It is less covered by the shrouds of clinical psychology and more available to the person on the street or a teacher in an ordinary classroom. Perhaps the greatest distinction lies in the work done developmentally. Those who develop emotional intelligence work at developing the set of abilities that underpin effective emotional functioning. Emotional literacy involves acquiring skills, attributes and competencies which together make us more emotionally competent. As the concept of emotional literacy has caught the imagination of educators and educational systems, so the links with other allied work has become clear. Proponents of Circle Time, for instance, (a group process that encourages open communication and boosts the self esteem of those that take part) have always been aware of the ways in which the circle processes and activities develop emotional competence and social skills (Bliss and Robinson, 1993; Bliss et al, 1995; Mosley 1993, 1996; Mosley and Tew, 1998; Smith, 2003, 2004; White 1990, 1991).

Peter Sharp, an educational psychologist, was one of the forerunners of emotional literacy in education. He worked for many years to bring emotional literacy into the education system throughout the whole

Local Education Authority of Southampton. He started by highlighting the need for emotional literacy at the level of the officers of the local authority and then slowly introduced the emotionally literate principles to many headteachers, teachers, schools and students (Sharp, 2001).

To the non-academic, the semantics associated with different streams of emotional literacy can seem somewhat obtuse. Perhaps for educators, a more interesting and relevant line of enquiry has been the debate about the importance of social and emotional factors in learning.

Social and emotional aspects of learning

In the words of Claude Steiner, 'emotional literacy is made up of three abilities: the ability to understand your emotions, the ability to listen to others and empathize with their emotions, and the ability to express emotions productively' (Steiner, 1997 p11). People who are emotionally literate have personal power, which means they are in command of themselves. They interact with other people in productive and positive ways which enhance self-esteem and emotional wellbeing. Theirs is an optimistic outlook. They have energy to struggle with the more difficult challenges that life brings. Emotional literacy improves relationships, makes cooperative work possible and creates possibilities between people. In a classroom, emotionally literate adults and children facilitate the development of a learning community. When people have a positive sense of themselves they are more open to new experiences, more flexible and willing to embrace change and therefore more able to learn.

The links between social and emotional development and learning have been embraced at a national level by the recent National Strategy for promoting Social and Emotional Aspects of Learning (SEAL). Materials were produced for primary schools in 2005 and for secondary schools in 2007.

The SEAL documentation states that 'children with good skills' in the social and emotional aspects of learning are 'more likely to be successful learners, make and sustain friendships, and resolve problems and conflicts fairly an defectively. They will be better equipped to manage their feelings, overcome difficulties and work and play cooperatively' (DfES, 2005).

Both the primary and secondary materials focus on the following five social and emotional aspects of learning:

- ▶ self-awareness
- ▶ managing feelings
- ▶ motivation
- ▶ empathy
- ▶ social skills.

In the primary sector, the materials are organised into seven themes: New Beginnings, Getting On and Falling Out, Say No To Bullying, Going for Goals!, Good to be Me, Relationships and Changes. Each theme is designed for a whole-school approach and includes a whole-school assembly and suggested follow-up activities in all areas of the curriculum. The materials build on effective work already in place in many primary schools and pay systematic attention to the social and emotional aspects of learning through whole-school ethos, initiatives such as Circle Time or buddy schemes taught PSHE (Personal, Social and Health Education) and Citizenship curriculum (http://bandapilot.org.uk).

The secondary materials are also structured around the five social and emotional aspects of learning shown above. Implementation strategies are left to individual secondary schools to give them the freedom to link with other initiatives such as the Every Child Matters Agenda, Healthy Schools, PSHE, Assessment for Learning, Including, Personalised Learning, Emotional Health and Wellbeing and Thinking Skills. The work outlined in this book forms an essential part of a school's approach to looking at the social and emotional aspects of learning because it highlights these very issues from the perspective of the learners themselves.

Summary

In this section you have:

► read the background to this work

► understood what students think school success means

► gained insights into a school student's lifeworld

► seen the framework that will be used throughout this book.

Section Two

Developing Emotional Literacy in School

In this section you will discover:

▶ how teachers act as role models for students   ▶ ways in which teachers facilitate student learning

▶ how to set a constructive classroom climate

▶ teaching approaches for exploring domains and constructs use in order to be effective in school.

In the first section of this book, we established not only that emotional literacy is an important factor in learning but also that the students recognised these skills at the heart of being able to do well at school. Perhaps we should not be surprised that the students' perceptions match those recently highlighted by research into emotional literacy (Goleman 1996, 1998; Gottman, 1998; Seligman, 1990; Steiner, 1977) and have been taken up by initiatives such as SEBS and SEAL, but it is always very reassuring to know that the adult's external view concurs with the students' internal view of the same phenomenon. Whichever way we look at the students' core construing, they put social, emotional and behavioural aspects of learning at the centre of the school enterprise. So the next question becomes how to work with students to enable them to develop these skills in a meaningful way in school so that they have the very best chance of doing well. This section presents the principles that I, and other researchers and practitioners, have found work when drawing young people into the discussions and experiential work that are foundational to developing the skills and competencies that comprise the social, emotional and behavioural aspects of learning.

We will cover the role of the teacher and teaching approaches.

The teacher as role-model

From the time they are born, young people learn by imitation. This mimetic learning, means that students respond most strongly to and are most likely to learn the qualities that adults model rather than the ones they overtly teach. Albert Schweitzer is reported to have said, 'Example is not the main thing in influencing others, it is the only thing'.

If teachers are going to help students to develop their emotional literacy, it helps if the teacher develops their own emotional literacy. The more aware we, as adults, can become of our own flow of emotional states as they continue throughout the day, the better placed we will be to understand and manage our feelings and recognise similar feelings in others. Similarly, if we find helpful ways to monitor and control our moods and discover the way in which some feeling states enhance our thinking and motivation, we will be better placed to encourage young people to develop these same skills.

Alongside an increased self-awareness in relation to emotions and emotional self-control, Carl Rogers, an eminent psychotherapist, identified three core conditions necessary for personal growth and learning to take place. These are: congruence, sometimes called genuineness; empathy, which involves a non-judgemental attitude; and prizing or unconditional acceptance, which accepts students as they are (Rogers, 1986a). It is very helpful to develop at least a 'good enough' measure of these qualities in ourselves so that we can facilitate the most productive classroom environment for personal and social growth and development. Please note, however that developing these qualities in ourselves may require some of us to lay down some of our more traditionally 'teacherly' qualities.

Teacher as facilitator of learning

Some teachers find it difficult to let go of the need to be the teacher in a classroom with an associated need to be in control and know the answers. There are times when teachers have to know the answers and others when they have to be very firmly in control of the classroom situation. Yet a lesson that explores some aspect of emotional literacy is not the time for thinking that they know any better than their students what the answers might be. This is the time for teachers to become facilitators of learning rather than deliverers of knowledge. The emphasis shifts from a teacher-centred approach in which he or she asks questions such as, 'What do the students need to know about this subject?' 'How can I plan a curriculum that covers the main subject matter?' 'How can I teach in such a way that students will gain the knowledge that they need?' to a student-centred approach that asks questions such as, 'What do you want to learn about this subject?' 'What are you curious about?' 'What issues concern you?' When teachers become facilitators of learning in this way, they take account of the individual's unique perspective on any event. The problem with social and emotional situations and events is that my perception of a situation or event will be different from yours and neither of us will be wrong. Both of us are right given our internal state, social and emotional history and cognitive abilities. It is really easy for us as teachers to negate a child's reality. Adults say things like, 'Don't be silly, of course it isn't like that' or, 'I don't think Lena would say that' or, 'Your imagination does run away with you' and so on. These kinds of statement easily cause a child to think that their perception is not valid, so they won't talk honestly about how they experience life, but give the information they think the adult wants to hear.

Genuineness

The first and most fundamental attitude that facilitates personal growth and change is congruence. Other words used for congruence are genuineness, reality and authenticity.

Congruence is a state of being that does away with facades or any attempt to hide behind a professional role so that we are genuinely true to ourselves. We can all remember times when a parent is listening to a child describe an incident at school. After a while, the parent's eyes glaze over yet they keep nodding and making affirming noises. It is only a few moments before the child notices the parent's lack of attention and says, 'You aren't listening'. How often does the parent say, 'Yes I am, I heard every word, carry on dear'? This is an example of non-congruence. If the parent had said, 'You are right, I had drifted off there. I didn't really know the people you were talking about. You'll have to take some time to explain who the people are,' that would have been a congruent response. Congruence can take more energy than pretending that we understand or are following. It is a difficult state of being to sustain for busy teachers, yet a student is unlikely to change a strongly held attitude, personal belief or behaviour if they think the significant adult in the situation is not giving them a genuine, honest response.

When a teacher is congruent in the classroom situation, they are aware of their own internal feelings in relation to what a student has said. The problem with being in touch with our feelings is that students can say things that cause us to have difficult or negative feelings. They may talk about a death in the family which triggers our own unresolved grief, or about situations involving illegal activities that send us into panic about child protection and how to deal with it. Congruence does not mean that we have to say what we are feeling or that we respond out of our internal state. It is much more about being aware of the feelings, being able to name them, to communicate them if it is appropriate and to use them to help us to listen more empathically to the students' lived realities. We can then take time to decide what we will do with difficult, sensitive or disturbing information at a later time, outside the confines of the lesson we are in. Neither does congruence mean that we have to disclose personal information about ourselves. Apart from anything else, young people don't want to hear endless stories from our past experiences. Some self-disclosure can be both interesting and instructional, but only in moderation.

Congruence or genuineness is important because it enhances the quality of relationships in the classroom and makes it easier for the students to trust the teacher. This in turn facilitates discussion about social, emotional and behaviour issues. When the teacher is congruent, the student will experience the discussion as open and honest and will not think that the teacher is trying to manipulate him. A lack of perceived manipulation makes it much easier for students to look at their own thinking, feelings and behaviour and to consider change. Congruence produces a more egalitarian classroom climate where the teacher is not wielding the power of superior knowledge when discussing issues relating to emotional literacy. If the teacher acknowledges confusion, apology and weakness, it can introduce new possibilities for students who may spend their lives in fear of weakness and confusion. Perhaps the greatest significance of congruence is that the teacher is modelling the very qualities he wants the student to acquire. We want students to become more self-aware, better able to identify and name their feelings, and so manage them and use them for productive relating and learning. These skills require the students to be more congruent themselves. If teachers are congruent, the students can learn by observation how to be more genuine too.

Empathy

The second condition that Rogers identified as important to facilitating students in making the subtle changes in self-concept which make for positive development is empathy.

Empathy involves the ability to see the world from another person's perspective.

It affords the other person the freedom to acknowledge how it is for him or her now, without someone judging that perception as foolish, inaccurate or juvenile. The person listening in an empathic way validates the view by communicating that they can see the situation the way the other person sees it. An ability to be empathic does not, however, mean that you have to abandon your way of viewing the world, agree with my way of viewing the world or even think mine is an accurate perception. What you do have to do is acknowledge my way of seeing and take some time to get inside my viewpoint to see what my world must be like if you saw it the way I do.

Whereas the profound level of empathy such as that practised by experienced counsellors is probably unrealistic for a classroom teacher, a good degree of empathy is essential to getting the best out of student conversations as they explore their emotional literacy and develop social, emotional and behavioural skills. Becoming non-judgemental and uncritical is one of the hardest changes for traditional teachers to make and a good starting point is working on not voicing (or showing by bodily responses) our first reaction to the things students say. Slow down the thinking and response time. Separate your personal view on the subject from the view you are hearing. Practise greater curiosity and ask questions to explore the student's story or view until you have a clear understanding of the way they are viewing it.

Acceptance

The third condition that Rogers highlighted for personal growth and change is variously called acceptance or unconditional positive regard. This acceptance or prizing is crucially important to a students' acceptance of themselves, which becomes the bedrock from which change can take place. We live in a world where people are boxed, labelled, pigeonholed and stereotyped. School is no exception. Students are labelled in a variety of ways. Labels can include 'hard working', 'bone idle', 'clever', 'disruptive', 'talented', 'air head' and so on. Once a label is given it is very difficult for the student to behave outside the label or for the adults to give the student the chance to behave in any way that would challenge their label. Acceptance requires us to lay aside our preconceived ideas, former experiences of this person, prejudices, stereotypes and labels. It is an attitude held by the adult that positively values the student for who they are. This value continues regardless of what the student does and is evidenced in seeing them afresh every time you meet.

When a student has not received unconditional acceptance from significant adults in their lives, they expect to be accepted only if they behave in ways that are approved of. For many students this has resulted in a lack of self-acceptance. They are fragile and self-protective or defensive in relation to other people. They may appear weak, inappropriately aggressive, unemotional or withdrawn.

Defended teenagers are like a fortified castle. They have the drawbridge of their personal castle pulled up and they repel all attempts to negotiate entry by metaphorically pouring boiling oil over the castle sides and sending arrows at the visitors. They can be very difficult, prickly, verbally aggressive or withdrawn. Providing unconditional positive regard or non-possessive warmth and respect breaks into the student's defensive protection.

We can, perhaps, all think of one student who was very difficult and challenging for a long time. Then we found a way to relate which had a dramatic effect on the student's defences. They let down the drawbridge, stopped sending out arrows and boiling oil and allowed us to enter the castle. It is probable that if we trace back what we did that made the difference, it will have been because of communicated unconditional acceptance over a period of time. It is not easy, however. Unconditional positive regard is hard for teachers to sustain in the hurly burly of school life when behaviour is often very challenging. Carefully prepared lessons can so easily be destroyed by the behaviour of a minority. It is important though, particularly when talking about personal, social and emotional issues, and teachers need to be able to afford their students a good measure of unconditional positive regard in order to create the conditions for personal growth and change.

This kind of response is often summarised as showing we like and accept the person even if we don't like the behaviour they are displaying. If this is impossible for a particular individual, it might be better to find another adult who has relationship with the student to work with him or her, such as a mentor, special needs teacher, school counsellor or teaching assistant. It is also worth remembering that a fragile student that lets down his or her defences will subsequently feel very vulnerable and may pull up the drawbridge again next time you meet. It may take several occasions where the student oscillates between highly defended and more open and vulnerable before they decide it is safe enough to leave the drawbridge down over a protracted period of time.

Setting the classroom climate

We have seen that the first key to exploring students' personal and social realities is where the teacher embodies the qualities of acceptance, genuineness and empathy. The second key is creating a classroom climate that is conducive to an honest exchange of ideas. If the climate is not right, students become defensive. They put up barriers to protect their self-image. They rigidly cling on to their current thinking and are not open to change.

No matter what the age of the child, the classroom climate is set by the adults in it, most importantly, the teacher. I remember when we had four teenagers in our home and I came in from work tired, fractious and unreasonable. Even before I opened my mouth, the children were on the defensive. No matter what I said, they were quick with a smart reply. They had read my mood as I walked between the car and the front door and were ready for me. One day, I said, 'When you are in a bad mood, I have to be nice and find a way to help you out of it. When I'm in a bad mood, I still have to get to be nice first. Why can't you notice how I am feeling and help me to feel better after a difficult day at school?' But my question fell on deaf ears. I was the adult, they were the children and that was the order of things.

The children take their emotional cue from the adults around them. This is not to say that you have to be an emotional whiz kid in order to develop your class' emotional literacy. It just means that you need to be aware of the impact you are having on them and work on your own skills so that you can offer them warmth, empathy, appreciation and congruence. It would be better to say for instance, 'I'm really stressed today and in a bad mood,' than to pretend to be all right and not give a congruent response.

After the teacher, the next important factor in creating a good classroom climate for discussing personal, social and emotional issues is to ensure that the students treat one another with acceptance and respect.

This is difficult in a teenage culture that feeds on put-downs. If you listen to radio stations aimed at young people, or at comedy television programmes, and tune in to put-downs, you will find them everywhere. It is a way of relating; a 'norm' for the young people in school today. That it is a norm does not make it emotionally safe, however. Young people are just as emotionally vulnerable to being disrespected, derided, laughed at, dismissed and not taken seriously as they ever were. The hard truth is that teachers have to work harder to create an emotionally safe space in their classrooms than was the case twenty or so years ago. Perhaps teachers would be more motivated to put in the additional effort if they realised how much young people appreciate it when teachers take the time make their classrooms the emotionally safe places in which personal and social growth and learning can take place.

> 'People do talk about sensitive things and we all keep it to ourselves. At the beginning we didn't say what actually thought but now we do.' (Student aged 13)

Groundrules

Only when groundrules were agreed and enforced in a meaningful way did ridicule, unkind laughter and put-downs stop. Once the group was seen to be a safe place, honest opinions and perceptions became more common and the circle became a place to exchange meaningful views and opinions, connected to real feelings. The teachers said that once this happened it became possible to explore, challenge and even change opinions, values and attitudes. Teacher of PSHE.

The students in the same study said, 'We set up groundrules at the beginning of the year about keeping issues within the circle and people keep to them. We made groundrules by sitting in a circle and talking about them. They are written in the back of our PSHE books and they are constantly referred to.' (Student aged 13.)

On the other hand Year 10 students astutely noted, 'It's not just that people don't keep the rules. It's that they don't care about them if teachers don't enforce them. If the teacher lives them then it works.' (Student aged 15.)

Groundrules that become 'the way we do things round here' really help to set the right climate for emotionally safe and open discussion.

Groundrules need to be:

- ► made with the class
- ► recorded, displayed and lived
- ► constantly referred to and reinforced every lesson.

Teaching approaches for exploring domains and constructs

Before we get into the detail of what each construct means, what it looks like and how to develop it with students, I want to explore some general principles for working with this type of information. If you are a PSHE specialist, or have had a lot to do with emotional and social development, you might want to skip this section, or skim it very quickly. If, on the other hand, you are fairly new to this kind of work,

I have included this section to provide you with some approaches that really work and to help you avoid some of the major pitfalls that can arise.

Often the choice of approach is dictated by practical constraints such as size of room, type of furniture, classroom layout or time available. If, on the other hand, you have a free choice and don't have to work in a science lab or in a room with pillars in the centre, then you will be able to move the furniture out of the way at least some of the time. If this is impossible, consider booking an open space such as the drama studio or hall so that you can make use of the range of approaches presented here that encourage young people to develop personally, socially and emotionally.

Working cooperatively

Learning is primarily a social activity. It requires supportive learning relationships and a healthy level of challenge. It involves making personal meaning from information that is being presented by linking it to previous learning or experience, often in conversation with others. Learning has an emotional as well as a cognitive component and different learners approach their learning in different ways according to preferred learning styles.

PSHE and tutorial lessons are ideal opportunities to develop the skills of groupwork and so engage learners in their learning. An effective functioning group of whatever size pays attention to the learning style, communication style, ideas and experiences of all its members. It is structured in such a way that creative thinking is facilitated by the very act of taking part in group activities and tasks. Developing emotional literacy is greatly enhanced by being part of a group and learning to play an active role in it. This can be a group of two as in paired work, small groups of three to six students, larger groups or the whole class. All teachers are well placed to facilitate groupwork that draws attention to and practises the skills of participation. As the group learns to work together effectively so the likelihood of students experiencing a sense of connectedness and belonging is increased (Stanford and Stoate, 1990).

Circles and their power

Circle Time has been widely used as a whole class approach for positive behaviour and personal social development in the primary sector. As a democratic and creative process, it can be used to reflect on and discuss a wide range of issues affecting individuals, classes and the whole school community.

For the individual, it is intended to:

► enhance self-esteem

► encourage pupils to reflect on their experience and behaviour

► identify personal targets for improvement

► help pupils to regulate their responses

► enable pupils to develop positive social relationships with peers

► become more sensitive to and tolerant of others.

The proponents of Circle Time have written for the secondary sector for many years, but the approach has been more widely adopted by secondary schools over the past five years or so. Several leading writers have produced materials for secondary students, either as part of a transfer package to help students make a smooth transition from primary to secondary school or as an approach to personal and social education (Bliss and Tetley: 1993, 1995; Cowling and Vine: 2001, Mosley and Tew: 1998, Schilling, 1999; Smith, 2003a, 2003b, 2004; Tew et al, 2006).

'I learned not to be nasty, to share, co-operate, to wait until it's my turn to talk and to put my hand up.' (Student aged 11)

'We really listened to each other and if you don't want to say what you're feeling, you keep hold of it, but otherwise, you say it.' (Student aged 12)

One of the most powerful and instructional strategies available for exploring and developing emotional literacy is the circle session. There are several different ways of running circle sessions and a wealth of ideas for activities, strategies and approaches that the reader can draw on for developing emotional literacy. I do not intend to present the detail of Circle Time and how to facilitate a circle session here, as there are many other texts that will cover this material more fully. For further information on circles and how to run them read: Ballard: 1982, Bliss and Tetley: 1993, 1995; Bliss and Robinson, 1995; Curry and Bromfield: 1994, Mosley and Tew: 1998, Schilling, 1999; Tew et al, 2006; and White: 1990.

Facilitating a Circle Time session is not as easy as it looks; however it is well worth the effort and you will reap the benefits. It requires practice on the part of the teacher and skill on behalf of the students. Be patient with yourself and your class, remembering that the circle's power develops over time. When it is used effectively it creates an ideal forum for dialogue. Self-awareness increases for every member of the circle and there are opportunities to explore and manage feelings and moods, developing personal responsibility, empathy, communication and group interaction skills.

Discussion or dialogue?

Though individual reflection has a part to play in social and emotional development, at the heart of the process lie talking, listening and being listened to. This is not just one person speaking and the rest listening, however. There has to be a more equal sharing of ideas, perspectives, values, attitudes and perceptions in order for people to develop their emotional literacy. I am calling this kind of interaction 'dialogue' to distinguish it from the normal classroom discussions. In most classrooms, a subject is discussed by the teacher asking a question of the whole class. The students might explore the question in pairs or small groups and then they bring their findings back to the whole class. The teacher acts as the chair of the discussion. If paired work doesn't take place, students put up their hands to volunteer a point of view and the teacher selects who speaks, how many speak and in which order. I once heard a 14 year old student say, 'We were talking about smoking. I put up my hand and waited but she never asked for my point of view because she knows that I really like smoking.' The other problem with the kind of discussion that takes place with a teacher up front addressing a room full of students is that the young people can't see one another's faces. They are forced by the layout of the room to look at the teacher at the front. This makes it very difficult for them to 'read' their peer's reactions to what is being said. They would have to turn around to see their classmates at the same time as speaking to the adult at the front of the room, so they miss the bodily responses and facial expressions of their peers. When discussion is constrained in this way, it is not conducive to an open exchange of honest views. On the other hand, if the students are arranged in such a way that they can see the people they are talking to there is an altogether different quality of interaction. In this context it is possible for both views and values to be challenged in a respectful way and there is the possibility that people might change their mind and or their behaviour. The term dialogue has been used to describe the kind of speaking and listening that engages people emotionally at the same time as it stimulates their thinking (Park, 2001).

The distinctions between discussion, conversation and dialogue have been well articulated by Francis (2001). She said discussion may involve a competitive stand-off between views and conversation is generally a free-floating exchange of information. 'Dialogue, by contrast, is an active process of two or more people enquiring about and learning from the distinct perspectives of others, where there is a real, and exciting possibility that their own positions will shift as part of the process'. When learning utilises meaningful dialogues, students have a more significant experience in the classroom which leads to being better able to apply what has been learned in one area to other aspects of their studies and lives. Students become confident and motivated to learn. Their openness to ideas stimulates imagination, creativity and a sense of being empowered to make things happen.

For the teacher, there are some challenges in cultivating dialogue in a classroom. The first is that there are no certain outcomes. The open-ended nature of this activity runs counter to almost every other part of the teaching day. We are so used to teaching set bodies of information against learning outcomes, which are measured against specific assessment criteria, that dialogues can seem very scary and even suspicious. The second challenge is that if teachers are to facilitate learning through dialogues, they have to cease being dispensers of knowledge. Even if the teachers are comfortable with this change of role, the students can find it difficult to accept that the teacher doesn't know.

Once students get used to having dialogues and begin to share their knowledge, it is astonishing how much they already know. In developing emotional literacy you are drawing on their innate wisdom, life experience and existent knowledge. That then becomes the basis for practising more productive ways of being and behaving. It is worth noting though, that dialogue does not come naturally to any of us. We have to practise the skills of listening and we need to be able to see the people we are talking to.

Before any dialogue can take place it is important to ensure that:

- ▶ you have developed some groundrules for talking about potentially sensitive information

- ▶ students have they have had time to become familiar with the area of emotional literacy that you are going to discuss

- ▶ they understand what the area under discussion, e.g. optimism, confidence means

- ▶ the students are comfortable to share with other people in the group.

Continuum

Another really useful method of getting at people's perceptions, values and attitudes is to use a continuum.

The principle of the continuum is that one end of the room represents one extreme of a range of views and the other end of the room represents the opposite extreme. The space between the two extremes provides for gradations of opinion. Continua can run from totally agree to totally disagree, from 0% to 100%, from never to always, least to greatest and so on.

One way I have used the continuum is to discuss a particular construct such as staying on track, using anger well, optimism and so on. For instance, one end of the room was marked as 100% and the other end of the room as 0% for using anger well. Students were asked to stand on the line to show the score they would give themselves for this construct. How high a score would you give yourself for controlling your temper? If you think back over the last week, how well have you used your anger by controlling it when you thought you were going to lose your temper or by using it to help you to get something done? Would you give yourself a score near 0% or nearer to 100%?

Once they had placed themselves on the line, they were asked to explore the results in the following ways:

- ▶ Ask the people standing at the 100% end to say why they think they had a high score.

- ▶ Ask the people standing nearer the low end to say why they think they had a lower score.

- ▶ Give them a few minutes to talk in pairs or small groups and tell stories of actual examples of times when they did or did not show the skills and attributes of the construct.

- ▶ Ask the people at the lower end of the continuum to think of examples of times when they have shown the construct. For example, when exploring confidence, even though someone gave themselves a low score overall, they may be very confident in looking after a younger sibling, making the tea at home, walking the dog, going into town alone and so on.

- ▶ Ask the people at the high end of the continuum to think of any examples of times when they might not show the construct. For example, for confidence, when might they feel less confident? It could be going to a party on their own or playing a musical instrument in a talent show, and so on.

- ▶ After the discussion you can then ask people if they think their score might be different now that they have talked about the construct. Get them to move to the place that shows their score now.

- ▶ Ask them to move to their ideal score. Once there, describe to the person next to you one thing you would see yourself doing if you had this score.

► At the end of the discussion make a list of things that would be evidence of the construct for this group. For instance after a discussion on confidence, the class could produce a list of actions that would show that people were confident, such as being able to talk to the whole group or being able to take part in a class assembly.

Each person chooses one way in which they are going to develop their confidence in the next week so that they can bring back their success stories to the next lesson.

Storyboards

Storyboards help students to explore aspects of events that they may not have noticed immediately. In drawing the storyboard, they may become aware of patterns of behaviour and recurring sequences of events. Noticing the events raises self-awareness and can lead to thinking about how to change the events or what is missing, how language is used and what the incident means to them. When you use storyboards, either the students or the teacher thinks of an event that illustrates a particular aspect of emotional literacy, such as two friends falling out and getting angry with each other or a teacher getting cross with a student for being late to a lesson. The story of what happens is drawn a single frame at a time with the space below the drawing and speech bubbles to show what the characters are thinking, feeling, doing and saying.

	TEACHER	**STUDENT**
THINKING	My lesson is interrupted by Natasha again.	I'll be in trouble for being late. I'm cross with Mrs Price.
FEELING	Frustrated, and cross at the interruption.	Anxious about being late. Indignant about unfairness.
BEHAVING	Gets cross. Unnecessarily accuses Natasha.	Defensive and aggressive. Uses sharp voice.

Pictures do not need to be artistic. The object of the storyboard is to explore the action and interaction, so stick figures can be used and rudimentary scenes to give the impression of the setting. Either a group can create a story board between them or individuals can produce their own. It might be helpful for the teacher to model the process on the board at the beginning or have a storyboard that they have made before the lesson. It is helpful to make storyboards big with one frame per A4 sheet rather than small like a comic strip in an exercise book. The larger frames make it much easier to read the story to the whole class and so facilitate a fruitful discussion. It also means that different frames can be added or substituted and alternative endings can be developed.

Once the storyboards are produced, the stories can be read to the class. At each point of decision in the story, stop and ask if anyone can think of a different way of thinking, feeling or dealing with the situation. This generates a range of options for taking the story in different directions and arriving at different conclusions. It is important when leading these kinds of discussions to use open-ended questions, keeping your voice tone and body language open and neutral, so that you don't put your own opinion or interpretation into the discussion. As soon as the teacher has an opinion, it becomes the 'right answer' and then an open exploration of emotional literacy and alternative ways of dealing with situations dries up. As the students explore the incident a frame at a time and as they discuss alternative interpretations, types of thinking, emotional reactions and ways of responding, they will broaden their own emotional repertoire and have a greater pool of strategies to draw on next time they are faced with a similar situation.

An extension of this activity is to photocopy the first few frames that set the scene for the incident and then ask the class (working in pairs) to develop alternative endings. This can be done by exploring possible outcomes and working backwards. For instance, a student is late for a lesson, the teacher is angry. If the students think about possible outcomes they may think of things like:

- ▶ the student ends up in detention
- ▶ she gets on quietly with the lesson
- ▶ he is angry for the rest of the lesson and does no work
- ▶ she is angry and sent out later in the lesson
- ▶ he is resentful and talks to his friend about it during the lesson
- ▶ she waits until after the lesson and goes to a senior member of staff to complain about the teacher and so on.

For each outcome there is a story that begins with the student being late for the lesson and develops from there to the outcome. The thoughts, feelings and actions of each character can be explored using the storyboards which can be photocopied onto OHT transparencies or scanned into a computer and used with an interactive whiteboard.

Role play

One of the best ways of developing emotional literacy and thereby learning how to handle difficult situations is to practise with a friend. The pair pretends to be interacting in the troublesome situation. One person tries out different approaches and perfects their comments and responses. The other shows several ways the person (whoever she is pretending to be) might react to the statements. The second person in the pair also makes suggestions and gives encouragement.

Role play involves the whole person. It is not just an intellectual exploration of social and emotional situations as the storyboard can be, but it touches our own real emotional responses and gives us an opportunity to practise the skills. Some students may already be skilled and they will certainly vary in their aptitude to develop the skills they have or to acquire new ones. Yet we all, young and old, can learn new ways of dealing with situations. We can all become more emotionally literate with self-awareness and practice. Role playing is learning how we could handle a situation to get the best outcomes. It requires the role players to be as they really are and to work with the way they respond now. Students do not generally have the inhibitions and problems that adults have with role play and they often really enjoy 'getting into role' and working on different scenarios.

Some tips for role play

► Select a fairly easy situation to start with.

► Make sure the group is well briefed about the purpose of the role plays and the parts they should play.

► Give them time to practise before showing their pieces to the whole group.

► Once you have seen a role play through once, try some Forum Theatre techniques. Freeze the action and ask other members of the class to say how different characters might be thinking. Or ask the class to suggest alternative ways of thinking and responding to change the action and get the characters to try out the new scene.

Ensure you have backup

It is always wise when working with emotional issues to ensure that you have some additional help to call on if you need it. This could take the form of a school counsellor or school nurse who is willing to take people on if they need more private conversations or individual support than the open classroom permits. You also need to be familiar with the school policies for child protection and your school's child protection officer so that you can talk about any issues that cause you to be concerned.

It might be helpful to compile a list of outside agencies that are available to students in their own time such as helplines, youth counselling services, Connexions and so on. If these sources of help are displayed in the classroom, you can draw attention to them and students can look for additional support when and if they think they need it.

Summary

In this section you have:

► thought about the role and qualities of a teacher in developing emotional literacy

► looked at how to set the classroom climate for developing emotional literacy

► been introduced to a range of teaching approaches:

  • encouraging collaboration

  • creating dialogue

  • continuum

  • storyboards

  • role play.

———

Section Three

Getting to Grips with the Five Domains

In this section you will:

► gain an overview of the five domains of a school student's lifeworld

► explore the relationship between the five domains

► examine the domains one at a time, learning the constructs that belong to each one

► consider how to define and recognise each of the constructs.

The things students consider to be important to doing well in school divide up into five domains or areas. These are:

► an awareness of self

► self-control, particularly when angry

► understanding other people

► getting on with other people

► motivation.

Four of the five domains are sub-divided into smaller areas of personal or social functioning which, in the students' perception, are the main keys to being able to get on at school. Together these 12 constructs represent the internal, subjective lifeworld that students inhabit in school. They are therefore essential to being able to thrive in the school environment.

Domains in the lifeworld of school

Awareness of yourself

The first domain broadly has to do with a student's awareness and perception of self. It includes aspects of self-image and affects his or her self-esteem. The four constructs that fall into this domain are: confidence, optimism, integrity and imagination.

Self-control

This second domain relates to a young person's ability to control him- or herself. For students aged 11 to 14 the feeling that is most troublesome to them in the context of coping at school is anger in all its forms. They recognise the need to find better ways of dealing with the energy generated by the host of different emotions that can lead to anger such as frustration, injustice, helplessness, hurt, anxiety and fear. Even at this young age, they recognise the need to use their feelings to generate positive motivation in school rather than being rendered incapable of constructive action or productive thought by angry feelings. The construct in this domain was therefore called 'Using anger well' rather than controlling or managing anger.

Understanding others

This third domain has two aspects. The first involves empathy and having the ability to see things from someone else's point of view. The second is what the students call 'being helpful'. This has to do with a practical response to being empathic. So if a student can see the that a teacher is stressed or overloaded, they might offer to help in some way such as volunteering to take the register back to the office, put some books away or help with a wall display. Similarly if a student can see that one of their classmates isn't coping with life, 'being helpful' would measure the kind of response they offer. It might involve support such as going with them to meet someone, the dining room or to find a member of staff.

Getting along with others

The fourth domain is the one that relates to being able to live and work alongside other people. It contains three constructs, each of which describes an aspect of a student's ability to get along with peers. These are: communicating well, fitting in with other people and working together.

Motivation

The fifth and last domain is motivation. This has two aspects to it. The first is a student's ability to deal with distractions and internal de-motivators so that they can keep going. This could be to do with distracting activity in the classroom, with internal feelings such as boredom, frustration or disinterest or when the subject matter seems irrelevant.

The second aspect of motivation relates to keeping the school rules. The students call this construct 'staying on track'. It involves wearing the uniform correctly, obeying the codes of conduct of the school and generally keeping out of trouble.

Relationship between the five domains

The diagram overleaf shows a model of the way the five domains relate to each other. The first two, to the left of the diagram, relate to self-awareness and self-control, which are both aspects of a person's internal functioning. These equate to Howard Gardner's intrapersonal intelligence (Gardner 1983). The arrow goes from self-awareness to self-control because only when a person becomes aware of themselves, of their thinking and feeling, can they learn to take control over them in the way they act and behave. The second two domains lie to the right of the diagram and relate to a person's ability to understand and deal with the world outside himself. They equate with Gardner's interpersonal intelligence and include the ability to understand and relate to other people. Again the arrow goes from the top box of empathy to the bottom box of getting along with others or social skills. As a person develops empathy and understands the ways in which other people experience the world, so they are motivated to find ways of relating to a greater range of perceptions and dispositions. The ability to relate with people who function very differently from us calls for increasingly sophisticated social skills. Without empathy, social interaction is entirely about getting my needs met and my voice heard. When empathy enters the equation, a more balanced form of social interaction can take place.

In the middle lies the fifth domain, motivation. Motivation seems to draw on a person's self-awareness, their self-esteem and aspirations, their optimism and imagination. It also draws on their self-control and ability to 'hang in there' even when there are few immediate rewards. Motivation in learning requires people to cope with and regulate their response to frustration, boredom, anxiety, fear and confusion while bringing more helpful emotions such as calm, bravery, interest, acceptance, serenity and curiosity to bear, so that the learning process is enhanced.

The students do not see motivation as only about 'keeping going' when things get tough, however. Their understanding is that it was also about 'staying on track' within the social demands of a school situation. They do not think you can do well in school unless you have learned to live comfortably and considerately alongside a large number of other people in very close quarters.

Of the five domains, the two that the students construe as most important are self-awareness and getting along with other people. Together these form the main keys to getting the best out of school. Arguably, finding ways of helping young people to develop in these two areas would be the most powerful intervention a school could make in order to engage young people in their learning and thereby gain greater success.

The five domains of constructs belong together and relate to one another. The domains represent areas or territories on the map of students' understanding of how to be successful in school. This means that the divisions can seem arbitrary and the boundaries between territories are inevitably not very well marked. One area merges into the next. Nonetheless, dividing up the social and emotional territory into regions is helpful when it comes to trying to tackle some of the feelings, the underlying thinking and the consequential actions that can either help or hinder productive school life.

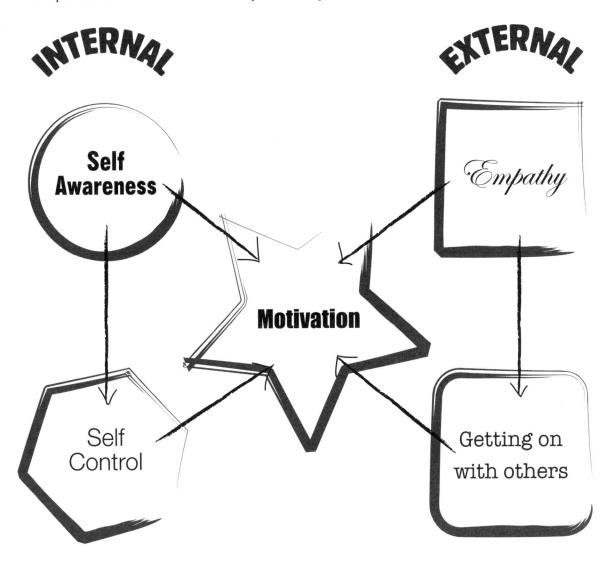

Domains and constructs one at a time

In the next few pages, we will look at the domains, and the constructs that belong in each, one at a time. Section Four provides student activities for each of the 12 constructs. The activities can also be found on the CD-ROM that accompanies this book so busy teachers can print them off and use them as they stand. On the other hand, you can use the information on the CD-ROM as the basis for a customised worksheet that suits your situation better. Section Seven gives the student handbook. Its pages have been developed with students aged 11 to 13 so that they can be easily understood by the age group.

Depending on the time available to you for exploring emotional literacy with your students, you can do all the activities, or select some. You can do the activities in class time or make up a student booklet, using the student pages and some of the activities that the students use for homework as well as classwork. Remember, however, to refer to Section Two of the book when you begin to work with young people on their emotional literacy. It presents the principles that facilitate growth and development in these areas.

Domain One: Self-awareness

The constructs found in this domain are:

- ▶ Optimism
- ▶ Imagination
- ▶ Integrity
- ▶ Confidence.

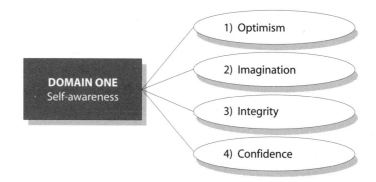

Optimism

Optimism is the ability to see life and situations in a positive light. It can be learned and taught to young people as long as the adult teacher herself sees the link between the way we think and emotional reactions that we have. Research into optimism has discovered four really helpful ways of dealing with difficult situations that enable someone to remain optimistic and resilient rather than defeated and depressed (Seligman, 1990, 1995). If you believe that optimism is an intrinsic character trait, a happy chance of heritage, it makes it hard for you to help someone else to change from a pessimistic to a more optimistic outlook on life. If you believe optimism can be learned, however, you can set about teaching the four skills that challenge pessimistic thinking and bring about a more optimistic view of life.

Skill One: Notice what you think

This begins by noticing the thoughts that flit through our minds when we are in a difficult situation or feeling bad. We have to learn to arrest the unhelpful thoughts so that we can change them rather than reacting automatically. For instance, a colleague borrows one of the department's videos to preview it and doesn't return it. You need the video for a lesson today and he is nowhere to be found. If you tend to think pessimistically, your automatic thoughts may be things like: 'This kind of thing always happens to me.' 'It's always my lessons that are scuppered.' 'I'll never be able to control that class without the video.' 'I don't have a single second to think of something else to do.'

Skill two: Decide if your thoughts are accurate

If our automatic thoughts are pessimistic and we habitually say unhelpful things to ourselves when we feel bad or when life events are difficult, we need to stop and evaluate their accuracy. The problem is that automatic thinking is not necessarily accurate. In order to challenge it, we have to gather evidence to prove or disprove our thoughts. For instance: Does this kind of thing always happen to you? When was the last time? How often in the past two or three weeks has a similar thing occurred? Is it true that your lesson is a complete write off without the video? Don't you have any other resources at all? Is it true that you won't be able to control the class? Can you think of a time when the class was fine without a video?

Skill three: Create a more accurate account of events

The next step in becoming more optimistic is to use the actual information to challenge the pessimistic thoughts and create a more balanced view of the current situation. For instance, there have been three incidents of not having the resources you needed for a lesson in the past three weeks. True they all fell in the last week, but that is only three lessons out of between 75 and 90. This is in reality between 1/25 and 1/30 of your total teaching time in those weeks.

Skill four: This is not a catastrophe!

Pessimistic thinkers tend to see life's difficult events in terms of disasters and catastrophes. The absence of the video is certainly a frustration and an annoyance and it will cost you effort and energy to sort out the lesson. This may well be energy that you simply do not feel that you have. But it is not a catastrophe or a total disaster and there are ways round it.

I once had a friend who was extremely pessimistic in social situations because of her own insecurities. In one period of time I forgot to meet her twice. The second instance was a dinner engagement that we had made. My own life was so fraught with small children and other demands on my time that I didn't record the engagement on the calendar, forgot to tell my husband and we didn't go. She jumped to the conclusion that I didn't want to know her anymore. Her automatic thinking was that she wasn't worth knowing, that there was nothing likeable about her and people always eventually discovered how useless she was. She thought that I was too embarrassed to say anything but I was fed up with her and no longer wanted her friendship. She didn't think to ring me up or ask what had happened. She sat in her home going over and over the same thoughts that confirmed her sense of rejection, isolation and depression. When I eventually rang her a few days later in the course or our normal friendship, I noticed she was very distant and cool and asked her what was the matter. Her reply flabbergasted me. She was so distraught about my perceived opinion of her that she was ready to move house and away from the area in order to avoid the pain. She had no strategies for challenging her automatic, pessimistic thoughts. A single event compounded a lifetime of pessimistic and catastrophic thinking so that her response was out of proportion to the event; huge and irrational. Optimistic people on the other hand, tend to handle one situation at a time, rather than thinking that everything is bleak when one thing goes wrong. They see difficult events as something they can deal with rather than blaming themselves and their lack of ability for the difficulties that come their way.

Identifying an optimistic person

People who are functioning optimistically can be identified because they are unlikely to get upset over small things. They tend to look for the best in people and situations and are likely to see difficulties as problems to solve rather than catastrophes to endure. Their knack of tackling one event at a time enables them to handle criticism and difficult feedback without getting upset. One of their skills is the ability to isolate a piece of feedback and keep it in perspective so that it continues to be feedback about one event, or one aspect of their personality or performance. These are people who have an internal voice that says, 'I made a mess of it this time,' rather than, 'I am a complete mess, a disaster waiting to happen!' When they get poor test results they say to themselves, 'I didn't do well in that one,' rather than, 'I am completely stupid and there's no way I'll ever do well.' When people think optimistically they welcome rather than dread feedback because it is a way of learning more about themselves. They are people who are confident that even if this time was a write off, they can find a way of improving next time.

Consequently, when people are being optimistic they are great to have around. They look on the bright side of situations and events and can usually see a way through difficulties to a better solution. They have a contagious up-beat outlook on life and are able to make people laugh, even when situations are difficult. Another feature of optimistic people is that they can usually find a way to look at things differently so that situations and events do not appear so bad. They can be very skilled at finding humour in a potentially difficult or stressful situation. The students said that optimistic peers are contagiously cheerful. They smile a lot, notice other people and greet them in a happy way. They unanimously enjoyed being taught by teachers who could be light-hearted and share a joke with them. It is worth noting that people who are usually optimistic can become more pessimistic in their outlook if they are overwhelmed by difficult life circumstances or if they are depressed or unwell.

Imagination

'There are no problems – only opportunities to be creative.' Dorye Roettger

Imagination lies behind creativity and creative thinking. It allows people to think differently and beyond the immediate situation they find themselves in. People with imagination can picture in their mind's eye how things might be; how they could change. They are people who think of possibilities rather than sticking with how it is now. In this sense, creativity is not the ability to create out of nothing, but a capacity to generate new ideas by combining, changing or reapplying existing ideas. Creative people see the links between things and put them into a new pattern. They like to use pictures, similes and metaphors when they think, talk and learn.

One of the most astonishing facts is that everyone has considerable creative ability, even the ones who say, 'There isn't a creative bone in my body. I'm purely practical'. Children are highly creative and the sad fact is that by the time they become adults, it has been schooled out of them (literally). Some recent research at the University of Bristol showed that the greatest casualty of our education system from age seven to 18 is creativity. It falls between the ages of seven and 11 and keeps on falling until the end of school (Deakin Crick et al, 2004). The good news is that the natural creativity of the young child can be reawakened. Often all that is needed is a commitment to being creative and some time allocated to it.

Part of creativity is an attitude which accepts change and newness. It is a willingness to play with ideas and possibilities. This requires us to be flexible in our outlook and to cultivate the habit of enjoying the good in the current situation while looking for ways to improve it. Creative people do not always tackle situations the same way. They are not stuck in a rut. They do not accept a narrow number of permitted or normal things, but push the boundaries and look for other possibilities.

Using imagination to be creative takes time, however. Rarely is a creative work produced fast. Creative people work hard and continually improve ideas and solutions. They make gradual refinements and alterations to their work. Here is the problem for our school system as it is today. There is so little time to cover a packed curriculum that we rush through the content, presenting it in one way and expecting everyone to access the information the way it is given. There is little time or space given to creative possibility and alternative solutions. Young people become fearful of 'getting it wrong' if they don't do it the set way, so they lose the capacity to play with ideas. At a conference in 2002, Professor Bart McGettrick from Glasgow University said, 'Covering the curriculum is the enemy of thought.' A sobering thought indeed.

There are several enemies of imagination and creativity which stop the creative flow at its conception.

Enemy number one: Over-reaction to a problem

Many people avoid or deny problems until it's too late, largely because they have never learned the appropriate emotional, psychological, and practical responses. The knack is to see a problem as an opportunity. The most creative people welcome and even seek out problems, meeting them as challenges and opportunities to improve things. Actively seeking problems and dealing with them constructively builds confidence, increases happiness, and gives better sense of control over life. When we understand the effect of problem-solving on self-efficacy, we begin to see why challenge programmes such as the Duke of Edinburgh's Award Scheme, among many others, has such a positive effect on students' confidence and personal growth. The impact of dealing with challenges in one area of life does not remain isolated in the student's experience. Rather it becomes generalised into an ability to keep a sense of proportion in the face of difficulties across a range of life experiences and a belief that they can find a way to solve problems.

Enemy number two: 'It can't be done'

People who say, 'It can't be done,' give in before they start and so create a self-fulfilling prophecy of defeat. Apparently running a mile in 4 minutes was physically impossible before Roger Bannister did it in 1954. The following year 37 more runners broke the record.

Enemy number three: 'I can't do it'

When people say, 'I can't do it,' they abdicate the process of trying. Their internal thinking tends to be along the lines of, 'Perhaps some other more creative or expert person could find a solution, but I can't because I'm not clever or skilled enough.' We all know the sort of student who throws down their pen and puts on a display of inappropriate behaviour from withdrawn sulking to shouting or aggression in the face of work that they don't think they can do. One 12 year old I taught used to come into the room, read the lesson objectives and look at the starter activity. If at the first glance she thought she couldn't do it, she would sit at her desk and refuse to get out her books. Yet some of our greatest inventions were made by people unqualified in the field. The ballpoint pen, for instance was invented by a printer's proof reader and two bicycle mechanics called the Wright brothers invented an aeroplane. If ordinary people have created extraordinary inventions, not one of us can say, 'I can't do it.' We just need an interest and commitment to the problem in order for creativity to have a chance.

Enemy number four: 'That's childish and what will people think'

In an effort to appear mature, sophisticated and 'cool', adults and young people often ridicule the playfulness needed for creativity. There is strong social pressure to conform and be ordinary and not creative. It matters that we free young people up to relax and let their individualistic creativity flow. Perhaps they need to know that people may talk about them and possibly laugh at them whatever they do, so why give up playfulness?

Enemy number five: 'I might fail'

The story is told of Thomas Edison who, in his search for the perfect filament for the incandescent lamp, tried anything he could think of, including whiskers from a friend's beard. In all, he tried about 1800 different ways of making a filament, using a lot of imagination and ingenuity. After about 1000 attempts someone asked him if he was frustrated by his lack of success and he said something along the lines of, 'No, I've learned a lot. I now know a thousand ways of not making a filament.' Young people harbour enormous fear of failure. They discover that the safest way to deal with their fear is not to try. For imagination to grow and develop, we have to help them to change the way they think about failure in order to see it as part of the creative process. In fact, failure and the risk of failure are intrinsic parts of the learning process so we have to make our classes places where students are praised for 'having a go' as much as for 'getting it right'.

Identifying imaginative people

These are the people in your class who make connections between bits of information in order to see things differently. If you are setting a problem-solving exercise, these are the ones who can come up with new ideas, different ways of tackling the problem, and new ways of doing familiar things. They can be quite irritating people, particularly if you want the whole class to do a particular task the same way. These are the students who will have a creative alternative (whether or not it is invited!). Their strong need to make connections between bits of learning in order to create a new pattern in their understanding can make them somewhat lateral and quirky in their thinking. Sometimes it is possible to dismiss them as being off task or irrelevant. On the other hand, they are great problem-solvers and often have some unusual ways of looking at things. They can think of several different ways to approach a problem or task. Their ability to employ imagination means that they are rarely stuck in a rut either in their relationships or their school work.

These are people who can think beyond the here and now into future possibilities. They can imagine good outcomes such as getting good marks, succeeding in sport or getting good exam results. They can imagine what it will feel like to do well and achieve so they tend to be people who make success happen. Similarly, they will work towards the imagined outcomes so they are not easily bored and can always think of creative ways to spend their time. There is always the danger that their creativity is not appropriate in the current situation, but that is a different issue!

Integrity

> 'Two things inspire me to awe – the starry heavens above and the moral universe within.'
> Albert Einstein

Integrity is defined as the quality of having high moral principles (Collins, 2004). This is a quality that the young people in my study saw as essential to doing well at school. Perhaps, had I probed further, I would have found that they view this as a quality essential to all of living and relating rather than one that is confined to life at school. Integrity, in the student's construing, involves two aspects. The first relates to personal integrity. It is part of their sense of self. This sort of integrity includes telling the truth and not lying in a variety of situations. Alongside truth went honesty in the form of not cheating and owning up to things that you have done, even if the consequences are unpleasant.

Honesty involves having the courage to do what is right even when it is difficult for you and being true to yourself even if your position runs against the mainstream view. The second part of integrity that the students identified pertains to social morality. This includes being trustworthy, keeping your promises and being careful with other people's business so you don't spread gossip or betray a trust.

It seems that developing integrity starts from inside the person and moves out into the social realm. The beginning of integrity is having a good sense of who you are, what you like and don't like, what you do and do not believe in. It then moves out to the social realm and what you would or would not do in any set of circumstances.

'Integrity needs no rules.' Albert Camus

Identifying people with integrity

These are students who take responsibility for themselves and their actions. They are honest and truthful about situations and events and very unlikely to involve other people or to blame them. They are OK about admitting what is true for them. They can wear clothes that are not in with the current trend or fashion, admit to liking music or TV programmes that are different from other people and have likes and preferences that other people don't agree with whilst still maintaining their place in the peer group. Despite being able to own to their individuality and differences, they tend not to alienate other people but leave them free to have their own individual likes and dislikes.

The students said that integrity is a very desirable asset in life. People with integrity make excellent friends. They will not gossip about other people and do not tell secrets. Similarly these people can apologise easily and will come back to say sorry so that relationships can be restored.

It is worth noting that the students did not always think it was advisable to tell the truth. They cited examples of times when it was unwise to be completely honest because the consequences were considered too severe. For instance one boy said that he would admit to breaking something in school but not at home because the punishment was less severe at school than at home.

Confidence

When the research that underlies this book was done, the strongest factors that contributed to doing well at school were the ones that relate to a sense of self. In particular, the students thought that being successful at school involved a good measure of self-confidence. A student who considers him or herself to be confident is comfortable in their own skin. This is a self-accepting person, at home with who they are at this stage of life. Self-confidence is an attitude which allows individuals to have positive yet realistic views of themselves and their situations. They trust their own abilities, have a general sense of control in their lives, and believe that, within reason, they will be able to do what they wish, plan, and expect. It is not that confident individuals will be able to do everything. It is more a measure of their ability to bounce back when some of their expectations are not met.

Confidence is born out of a good self-image and positive self-esteem. These are people who have received enough good messages about themselves to have a picture of themselves as capable, responsible and skilful people. They have a strong sense of themselves as individuals, separate from and yet in relationship with significant others. Because they feel good about themselves they evaluate themselves positively (high self-esteem) and do not feel the need to defend themselves against other people. These are people who tend to want to know how other people see them. They feel positive enough to deal with any negative feedback and strong enough to know that they can develop any skills that they are short on at the moment. Even when some of their expectations are not met, they continue to be positive and to accept themselves. These are people who are willing to risk the disapproval of others because they generally trust their own abilities. They don't feel they have to conform in order to be accepted.

In contrast with the confident person, those who lack self-confidence are over-dependent on other people's approval in order to feel good about themselves. These are the students who avoid taking risks because they fear failure. They generally do not expect to be successful. They often put themselves down saying things like, 'I'm stupid', 'I've never been good at maths' or, 'I won't do well you know.' They also tend to dismiss or ignore compliments and positive feedback that comes their way.

It is worth noting that self-confidence is not necessarily a general characteristic which pervades all aspects of a person's life. Typically, students will have some talent or area of their lives where they feel quite confident. This could be things like sporting ability, social skills, acting or music. At the same time they can feel lacking in confidence in other areas such as personal appearance, relationships or academic ability.

Developing confidence in itself is not enough to guarantee success, however. Confidence is just one of the 12 constructs that are important to doing well in school. Nonetheless, the data does support a view that increased self-awareness, essential to developing confidence, is the foundation stone on which all the other attributes and skills are built.

Identifying a confident person

These are the people that are good to have in a group or a class. They are happy to talk in front of the whole class, but without 'hogging' the limelight. They do not need to be the centre of attention, but they are happy to hold that position if it is required. They may not be the people that volunteer to report back from group work, because they may well take second place to their more needy, and lower self-esteem peers, but they are the ones that are the most capable of reporting back and who are most likely to give a report based on the findings of the whole group rather than promoting their own view above the others. Confident people are comfortable talking to a range of people including teachers and other adults. They present themselves confidently and speak clearly in a wide range of different situations. They tend to be aware of their own capabilities and they feel OK about themselves.

An interesting feature of confident people is that they can stand up to other people without falling out with them or getting into a fight. Similarly, they can stand up for their ideas without having to be either aggressive or defensive. They can work on their own and don't need others to tell them what to do all the time. On the other hand, they are happy to work with other people.

Domain Two: Self-control

The construct found in this domain is:

▶ Anger.

Using anger well

It was interesting to note that the only emotion that students identified as important to them in being able to do well in school was being able to deal with angry feelings. Other forms of self-control such as the ability to delay gratification, to wait for your turn, stand in a queue, be quiet, control body movement and so on didn't feature in the way students talked about the lifeworld of school. This tells us that the overriding issue faced by students in school between the ages of 11 and 14 is dealing with their anger. As young teenagers, they seem to find themselves angry often, for a variety of reasons and in many different ways. They find anger to be counter-productive to doing well at school and they need a repertoire of ways to recognise it and deal with it. The students seem to view anger as a bad thing; a negative force. In writing this material, I have chosen to turn that view around and rather than thinking about ways of eliminating anger, I have chosen to think about ways of using anger well.

Anger is often considered a negative and undesirable thing. Yet anger does not always have to be destructive. It can be very useful in providing the motivation and energy to get things sorted out or for changing something that is unjust or unfair. Anger itself is not a problem. The problem arises when anger is not used well and the pressure that builds up when we feel angry is not released safely.

Identifying people who can use anger well

These are students who can identify and talk about the difference between anger, frustration, hurt, disappointment and embarrassment. In other words, they can separate out inside themselves some of the main causes of angry feelings and give them an appropriate name. Similarly, they have a good vocabulary to talk about the strength of angry feelings from mildly annoyed or irritated to furious. (It is worth noting here that students who have done the SEAL work in their primary schools, may have already developed a good emotional vocabulary.) Students who have developed a breadth of language to talk about their angry feelings have often moved on to find ways to express them without destroying property or relationships with other people. These are people who can talk about how they feel rather than resorting to shouting abuse or swearing. They can stay connected with the difficult feelings inside themselves without either:

► turning the anger outwards and saying unkind things as a way of lashing out at another person or

► turning the anger inwards and hurting themselves. This could be physical harm or hurt such as eating disorders or cutting or it could be mental hurt such as depression.

The people who deal with anger best have realised that anger can provide energy to make them feel powerful to take action and make changes. They have found safe ways to let off steam or express their anger such as playing sport. Similarly, they have found appropriate ways of expressing their point of view or their objection to someone else's point of view in a way that is assertive and stops them having to lose their temper or get violent.

Domain Three: Understanding Other People

The two constructs that the students think describe understanding other people are:

► Empathy
► Being helpful.

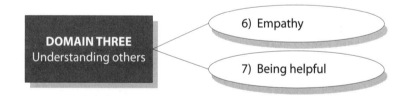

Empathy

In 1990 an academic called Jones conducted some research which asked the question, 'What are the characteristics of a capable, successful learner?' His research showed that successful learners are knowledgeable, self-determined, strategic, and empathetic (Jones 1990).

It is fascinating that Jones' research agrees with the view of the students in my study and supports the five domains. He found that in addition to having knowledge, including critical and creative faculties, successful learners need confidence about themselves as learners and motivation to learn. In addition they need insight into the motives, feelings, and behaviour of others with the ability to communicate this understanding (that is, empathy). Jones added to this list that successful learners also need tools and strategies for acquiring, evaluating, and applying knowledge. As the young people in my research so accurately identified, one of the essential ingredients to being successful in school is to be able to identify with other people's feelings and accurately communicate that understanding.

Empathy is often confused with sympathy. They are different however. Empathy is the ability to put yourself in someone else's shoes and view the world they way they would view it. Sympathy is being able to see someone else's situation and know what you would feel like if you were in that situation. Sympathy allows you to stay in your own skin and think how you always think. Empathy is much harder. It requires you to get out of your skin and into someone else's. Empathy is the only way we can truly understand someone else and it is a great skill for being able to negotiate well. It enables students to negotiate with parents or teachers when the student's view does not match up with that of the adult.

Jones noted that successful students often recognize that much of their success involves their ability to communicate with others. They are able to view themselves and the world they live in through other people's eyes, which includes examining the beliefs and circumstances of others. Successful students value sharing experiences with persons of different backgrounds as a means of enriching their lives (Jones 1990).

Identifying empathic people

These are students who are 'tuned in' to other people. They notice how other people, both fellow students and adults, are feeling. They are able to notice and recognise times when other people are behaving out of character. This skill involves a tendency to notice the small and sometimes subtle changes in other people's moods or behaviour and having a noticing mechanism that enables them to not to take other people's mood changes personally. Empathic people are more likely to be able to separate themselves from other people and recognise which feelings and which thinking belong to whom. They are better at knowing if a problem lies with the other person or whether it is something they should tackle themselves. They are very good at helping other people to sort things out and are less likely to withdraw or become hurt by other people's mood changes.

The students said that people with empathy get on well at school because they are great to have around. They do not think that they have caused other people's mood changes. They don't jump to conclusions but listen to other people's opinions and can make a wide range of people feel welcomed and included. Similarly, if there is trouble between individuals or groups of people, those with empathy can work out how both parties are thinking and feeling so they can often find a way of helping them to sort out the problem.

Being helpful

For the students in the study, empathy did not stop with an intellectual understanding of how other people think and feel. They were equally convinced that someone with empathy will respond to the other person. 'Being helpful' was the label they applied to the things that people did in response to having empathy with someone else's life situation. When people can understand how another person thinks or feels, they are more likely to be helpful to that person. Helpfulness is an outward expression of empathy in the students' lifeworld. The students noted that in order to do well at school, they had to be helpful to adults as well as peers. They talked about helping stressed teachers by giving out books, collecting in homework and taking the register back to the office. They also talked about helping their peers with aspects of school work, with social situations and with personal issues.

Identifying helpful people

These are people who genuinely want to help others. The main characteristic of their helpfulness is that it is neither boastful nor bigheaded. These are truly kind members of the school community who offer to help others in a wide variety of ways. They will go out of their way to help people who are stuck with their work. These are the people who have the measure of other people's skills. They also understand and are compassionate about the fears and weaknesses other people have, even if they don't experience life the same way themselves. They therefore go out of their way to ensure that other people do good work and do not make unnecessary mistakes. In social situations, helpful people will notice if someone is under-confident and will go with them when they have to go and see those in authority. They are similarly 'tuned in' to the isolated, lonely and unhappy. They will often hang around with people who are left out, even if they are not their friends, and look for ways to include them or integrate them into the wider group.

Domain Four: Getting Along with Other People

The three constructs that make up the domain called getting along with other people are:

► Working well together

► Fitting in

► Communicating well.

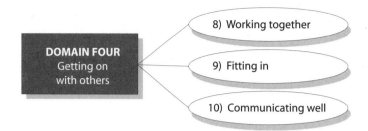

Working together

Over the last decade a great deal has been written about the academic and social benefits of co-operative learning. From a research perspective, the major finding has been that organizing learners into teams whose members differ from one another in race or ethnicity, gender, ability level, and other attributes, results in significantly greater pro-social interaction among these different learners (Johnson et al, 1983; Kohn 1991; and Slavin 1985). When they have participated in cooperative learning groups, students report and are observed to exhibit several beneficial attributes. They become more accepting and respectful towards other people, particularly those who are different from themselves. They therefore become increasingly able to relate to more kinds of people. They become better able to imagine other people's point of view and gain a greater appreciation of the different strengths that diverse people can bring to a learning group. Increased appreciation often leads to deeper cross-racial and cross-ethnic friendships.

Kohn (1991) writes, 'Cooperation is an essentially humanizing experience that predisposes participants to take a benevolent view of others. It allows them to transcend egocentric and objectifying postures and encourages trust, sensitivity, open communication and pro-social activity' (p. 504).

Findings in learning theory also indicate that learning is a social activity (Deakin Crick et al, 2004). Learning is enhanced by supportive learning relationships and a healthy level of challenge. It involves making personal meaning from information that is being presented by linking it to previous learning or experience, often in conversation with others. Learning has an emotional as well as a cognitive component and different learners approach their learning in different ways according to preferred learning styles. Groupwork is a major key to engaging learners in their learning. An effective, fully functioning group of whatever size pays attention to the learning style, communication style, ideas and experiences of all its members. It is structured in such a way that making meaning is facilitated by the very act of taking part in group activities and tasks. The students think that it is important to learn how to be part of an effective group. They believe that success at school is underpinned by opportunities to experience the sense of connectedness and belonging that come from a well-facilitated group process.

In every community we have to be able to work with other people. This is true in families, in clubs and societies and in school. Those who work in school are all too aware that in the world of work we also have to work in teams and responsibly do our bit in order to complete a bigger, more complex task. When people work in teams, each individual has to take responsibility for their own work and they each have to trust that the other members of the team will work equally hard. The students also see being able to work together as an essential ingredient to doing well in school. It is not that they think people can't get good exam grades unless they can work with other people. Rather they don't seem to be able to conceive of someone getting on well at school, being successful in the peer group, getting the best out of their school years and doing well in their exams without being able to work cooperatively with other people.

It is interesting to note that, from the students' perspective, a key part of working cooperatively is being able to share. In their construct called 'working together' there is a smaller, but clearly identified, group of ideas that relate to being generous with possessions and ideas. The need to be able to share is as relevant to family life as it is for school life. People who can't share make life difficult for themselves and for those around them. On the other hand, sharing requires a degree of trust. The students were clear that we have to be able to trust the other person to return money that they borrow and to look after possessions that they share. Unless the other person is trustworthy, sharing cannot take place.

Identifying those who work well with others

These are students who can manage to work well in any group task. They care about other people and tend to notice what they are good at so they encourage other members of the group to play their part in the overall project. They are very encouraging in a group situation and want everyone to do the best work they can so they make sure that everyone is doing the job that they are best at. They value the contribution that each person makes to the group and do not easily get either cross or frustrated. They work with the group rather than disrupting it. These are generally people who are generous-spirited. They will work in a group without dominating everyone else and without being selfish or hogging all the equipment. They will tend to look at the needs of everyone in a group or class and think about being fair with resources.

They don't take the best things without thinking about other people. These are also people who share their personal equipment such as pens and pencils, sharpeners and rulers and are willing to lend money to those who have forgotten it.

School work often calls for cooperation in a group or team situation. Students note that though people who share are good to have in a group and tend to get on well at school, they can also be taken for a ride by those who do not have much integrity. The student's view was that sharing needs to be tempered by wisdom about who you share with. They gave examples of times when they had lent a pen or a ruler to someone and the other person had broken it or failed to return it. In this example, they were very unwilling to lend things to that person again. The lack of sharing was not to do with an inability to work with other people, however. Rather it was evidence of exercising wisdom about the integrity of the other person.

Fitting in

According to the students, being able to fit in is extremely important in being able to function effectively in school. Those who can't find a way to fit in become isolated, miserable and even depressed. The motivational psychologist Maslow (1962) wrote about the same ideas in his hierarchy of human needs.

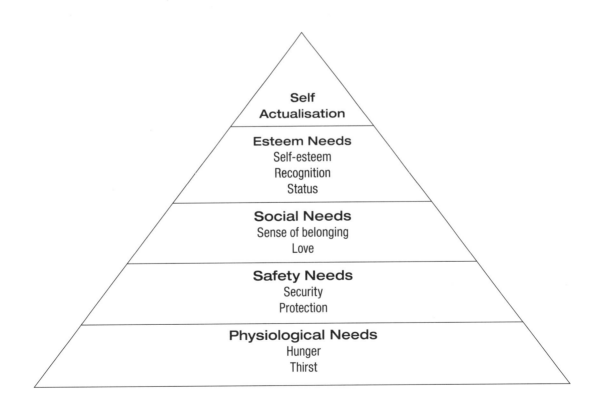

Maslow wrote that in order for someone to 'self-actualise' or reach their potential, their needs have to be met at each level of the hierarchy. At the most basic level, we all need physiological safety. That means enough to eat and drink and a place to shelter where we are neither too hot nor too cold. If our physiological needs are met, the next level of the hierarchy is the need for emotional safety. As human beings, we require emotional safety for psychological well-being. We need to know that there are at least some people who care about us, who want the best for us and are not going to harm us physically or mentally. Attention to physiological and emotional safety generates a sense of connectedness, affection and belonging in a group of people.

In a learning situation, Maslow's hierarchy applies. Students learn best when their physiological needs are met. This means they have had enough to eat and drink, the classroom is neither too hot and stuffy, nor too cold and they have access to a toilet. Emotionally, the climate has to be safe enough for them to risk making mistakes. If there is a fear of ridicule or put downs, they will not take the risk of making themselves vulnerable. Only when these conditions are in place can the students begin to feel connected with the adults and one another and so begin to gel as a community of learners. It therefore becomes everyone's responsibility (teachers, other adults in the school and all students) to ensure that people can fit in. This requires attention to equal opportunities, inclusion of diversity and different learning needs as well as to bullying issues and friendship groups so that people are not excluded. In my research, however, the students identified a set of skills that students needed if they were going to fit in easily.

Identifying people who can fit in

These are students who can get alongside other people without alienating them or making them feel awkward. They can fall in with other people or groups of people and 'go with the flow' without always having to have their own way. Since they don't need to have their own way all the time, they don't moan or make life difficult for everyone else if things are not going their way. They will adjust their plans to fit in with other people. They don't have to dominate conversations but can talk to anyone and join in any conversation. They are able to listen to both sides of an argument and are good at resolving conflict. They have good empathy skills and can see things from different perspectives. They can stay cool so that they can help people who are arguing to sort things out.

Communicating well

A little-recognized value of listening and inquiring relates to the realization that in human relationships, it is frequently not what the facts are, but what people think the facts are which is truly important. There is benefit in learning what someone else's concept of the reality of the situation is, no matter how wrong it might be.

Bryan Bell

Educators are communicators by definition. They have to be able to communicate knowledge, understanding, concepts and ideals. Good communication is a highly-prized skill at all stages of life. Students need to understand that good communication skills become even more highly sought as people leave education and enter the world of work. It is the skill of communication that makes the work situation a more comfortable and productive place. In the research, the students show that they too understand that good communicators oil the wheels of school success. These are the people who can make and keep friendships. They are able to negotiate making and breaking friends and can keep relationships healthy over longer periods of time. They can work in teams, represent themselves and represent other people well.

Identifying good communicators

These are people who are good at both speaking and listening. They are able to actively listen so they truly hear what other people are saying. They tend to demonstrate that they have heard by making non-verbal responses to the things they hear such as nodding their head and giving appropriate eye contact. They also provide helpful comments about what they have heard, or give a summary of it so that the other person knows that they have been understood. These are people who do not shout out inappropriately, talk over the top of others or interrupt them when they are speaking. They can choose the right kind of talking (appropriate vocabulary, tone of voice, subject matter, volume) to fit any situation they find themselves in. They do not interrupt other people by speaking before the other person has finished speaking their last sentence.

Domain Five: Motivation

The constructs found in this domain are:

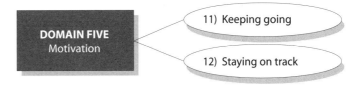

▶ Keeping going with work

▶ Staying on track with the school.

Keeping going with work

In the research, the students knew without a shadow of doubt that the ability to keep going with work, or internal motivation, was a major key to doing well at school. They noted that motivated people achieve better than demotivated ones and that motivation gives a dynamic to students that enables them to do well in a more general sense than purely academic achievement.

There has been a lot of research into motivation in the past ten or 15 years (Deci and Ryan, 1991; Dwek, 1999; Seligman, 1995; Smith, 1998). If we could find a formula for motivating young people, the job of education would be much easier and the success rate much higher. The dominant finding of the research is that motivation is a complex and multi-faceted attribution however. Causes of demotivation vary from person to person and there is no universal trigger that is guaranteed to motivate them. Nonetheless, there are some underlying principles that are helpful in addressing low motivation in young people.

According to Carol Dwek, an eminent psychologist working in the field of education, one of the major causes of demotivation in school is a belief that students with high ability are more likely to do well than those with who are less clever. This belief can be held by both adults and children. The students think, 'If I am not very clever, I am therefore not going to do very well, so I might as well not try.' The adults (including teachers) may believe that high ability will result in high grades. They therefore expect more from the young people of higher ability and the expectation can become its own self-fulfilling prophecy (Dwek, 1999). It is probable that all teachers can call to mind some young people who have very high ability but are so worried by the prospect of failure, or so under-confident about their ability, that they give up when they hit any obstacle or difficulty. Sometimes they refuse to try so that they do not have to risk either failing or having their worst fears realised. On the other hand, we can probably all cite lower ability students who by dogged effort and adherence to advice have managed to do very well at school. So what makes the difference?

The first set of students (and adults) believe that intelligence is a fixed commodity. They think that we were all meted out with a set amount by the genetic lottery and there is nothing we can do about it. When failure or difficulty comes along they respond by showing helplessness. They experience negative emotions, denigrate their intelligence, see no way of making the situation better, reduce their persistence and so lower their expectations. Because their belief system says the amount of intelligence I have is the key to success, any failure must mean a lack of intelligence. Similarly since intelligence is a fixed commodity, I can't do anything about it and I might as well give in.

The second believe that effort rather than ability is the key to success. They see learning as an incremental process which can be mastered. Intelligence is therefore not a fixed entity but an incremental, malleable quality that can be increased. They have a robust attitude to failure and stay focussed on the successful end, in spite of the present difficulties. When this group of students encounter failure they don't blame their lack of intelligence. They don't blame anything. They don't look for reasons for the failure or even consider that they were failing. They seem to see the current setback as a problem to be solved or an obstacle to overcome. Rather than give in to helplessness, this group start to look for ways to improve their performance (Dwek, 1999).

There is a certain amount of confusion in the teaching world about the relationship between success, motivation and praise at the present time. Many adults believe that guaranteeing success will provide the incentive and drive to try again and to go for a more difficult task next time. Many also believe that praising children will boost their self-esteem and so motivate them to greater success.

The research suggests that confidence and success are not, in themselves, the answer to motivation when the going gets tough. The confidence students bring to a situation often doesn't help them when they meet with difficulty if they believe that intelligence is the key to success. The problem with believing that intelligence is the key to success is that the flip side of this belief is failure must mean lack of intelligence. Or in other words, if I fail, I must be thick. If we add to this another belief that intelligence is fixed then I am doomed to fail, not only this time but every time, because I am thick. These beliefs become a double bind. If I fail I must be thick. If I'm thick I'm bound to fail. No amount of praise for my intelligence will change my belief and motivate me to try again.

A focus on academic intelligence is fatally flawed for motivation, especially as any measure of intelligence measures what I can do right now. It does not measure my potential. Surely we have all met people who were deemed to be failures at school. They were the ones who achieved very little and were often overlooked or in trouble. Then you meet them ten years on and they are successful business men and women, entrepreneurs and leaders. If you probe further, you will probably find that they went back to education in their twenties and have been highly successful in their chosen area. So what happened? Did they suddenly gain intelligence or did they switch on motivation and a belief that they could achieve no matter what they were told at school?

In the light of the findings cited above, we see that increasing student's motivation involves challenging beliefs, both ours and theirs. It means praising their incremental mastery of knowledge and tasks and encouraging the effort each step involves.

Identifying a motivated person

These are students who keep going even when they find a piece of work or an activity difficult. They do not give up easily because they know that if they keep trying, they will eventually succeed. They cope well with some of the difficult feelings that can result from finding a task hard, such as frustration, irritation, anxiety, hopelessness and even boredom. These students are good at ignoring distractions from other people or other classroom activities. They stay focussed on the task they are doing and like to finish work. They get a sense of satisfaction and experience themselves in a positive way (higher self-esteem) when they have done a job well.

Staying on track with the school

Staying on track is to do with the keeping and breaking of rules It is the form of motivation that is important to being a member of a wider school community so that a large number of people can live and work together in a relatively confined space. The students are clear that people who can't or don't stay on track with the school rules and codes of behaviour end up in trouble. However, they were equally clear that slavish adherence to every rule makes you extremely unpopular. In fact, they would go so far as to say that it is unnecessary. They identified a middle path where people kept most of the rules most of the time and occasionally broke one, usually when there was little risk of major harm or trouble. I guess it is the same as in the adult world. How many of us slavishly keep to the speed limits at all times and in all places? Most of us, if we are honest, keep roughly to the speed limit most of the time and carefully within it if we know there is a speed camera or police speed trap. On the other hand, we drive with extreme caution if there is a dangerous situation or if we are at risk of hurting ourselves, our passengers or other people. That was the way the students viewed school rules. They understood that those who know how to stay on track (to keep and break the rules in such a way that they don't cause harm, damage or conflict) find school life much easier and more pleasant.

One student said, 'We have a one way system in our school. When I am late for a lesson, I check no one is looking and dodge up the stairs the wrong way because it is such a long way round the one way system. I don't think that breaking that rule is a bad thing. It means that I get to the lesson quicker.'

Identifying those who are good at staying on track

These are the students who are able to see the bigger picture. They have thought about the need for rules and codes of behaviour in order for a lot of people to work and move in a school. They have empathy for the adults in the school and their need to keep students safe from accidents and incidents. These are also the more self-controlled individuals of your school. They can control their impulses and don't run, scream and shout in corridors. They can walk around the buildings in a calm way. They can also wait their turn in a classroom situation and don't get too frustrated by the time it takes for a teacher to give attention to 25 or 30 people. These are young people whose needs are probably being met in other aspects of their lives so their demand level is reduced in the classroom context. Maybe they learned better control over their emotional states when they were younger so that their ability to tolerate frustration, anxiety, fear, anticipation, excitement, boredom and so on is high. Their less fortunate peers, who have not had good earlier experiences or who have a lower tolerance threshold, may find it altogether more difficult to stay on track in school. These are people who need to develop a greater self-awareness and more self-control.

Summary

In this section you have:

► learned about the five domains that students use in order to be effective in school

► seen how the five domains link with each other

► looked at the twelve constructs and seen how they fit into each of the domains

► been introduced to definitions of each of the twelve constructs

► considered how to identify the twelve constructs in students.

Section Four

Classroom Activities to Develop Each Construct

In this section you will:

▶ be introduced to adult notes on how to develop each of the twelve constructs

▶ be given practical classroom activities to develop each of the twelve constructs.

This section presents classroom activities for each of the 12 constructs. The material is arranged with adult notes and student activities. The proportion of each varies depending on the demands of the construct. Sometimes a construct has a lot of adult notes that explain how a teacher or other adults in the situation can encourage students to develop the qualities and skills needed, sometimes there are very few. In developing confidence, for instance, there are many activities that adults can lead and facilitate to increase individual and group confidence without using student worksheets or other resources. In other constructs such as integrity, the adult notes are brief and the most of the developmental work is presented as student activities. Whether the activities are adult led or completed by the students with little help from the adult, it is often helpful to bring the discussion to a conclusion with some feedback to the whole group. Ideally the whole group feedback is run as a circle so that each person can see each of the other faces and judge how their contribution is being heard and received. Returning to the whole group for the plenary has many benefits, including increased psychological connection, greater willingness to be vulnerable to the group, a summary of the learning, an opportunity to voice new insights, a felt sense of connection in the group and a platform for higher quality dialogue in the next lesson.

Self-awareness

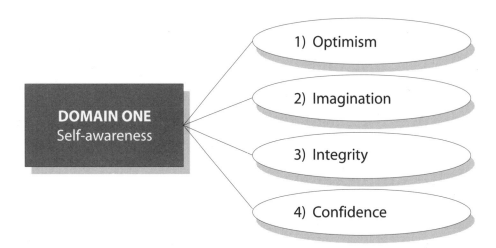

1) Developing Optimism

Adult notes

Encouraging your students to change pessimistic thinking to more optimistic thinking will take time. They have to first become aware of their automatic thinking patterns, and then learn to challenge the thinking before creating more optimistic alternatives (see Section Three). You as the adult in the situation can be a powerful role-model for thinking optimistically and this means that you have to:

- ▶ notice what you think automatically
- ▶ decide if your thoughts are an accurate account of events
- ▶ create a more accurate explanation of what is going on and
- ▶ decatastrophize the situation.

The student activities given here are to increase students' awareness of pessimistic and optimistic thinking. They can be used on their own or form the basis of more extensive work. It might help to have a section of the classroom display given over to developing emotional literacy. You could look at a construct a week over a term or so and build awareness by drawing attention to each construct regularly in the general business of classroom life.

How to Think Optimistically

	Optimistic people		Pessimistic people
T	See events as Temporary (sometimes happens)	P	See events as Permanent (always happens)
S	See events as Specific (happened on this occasion)	G	See events as Global (always happens)
BB	Blame themselves for their Behaviour in this event	BG	Blame themselves Generally

Work in pairs. Look at the table. Several different kinds of thinking are given about events. Decide which kind of thinking each represents and write the correct code next to it.

What do they think?		
Event	**Optimistic person**	**Pessimistic person**
Get a bad test score even when you revised	It was a difficult paper. I didn't read the questions properly. I wasn't on top form. I can do better next time.	I'll never be able to get a good test score so there is no point in trying. I'm just thick. I'm no good.
Your friend Sam didn't meet you in the usual place so have to walk to school alone	Something must have come up for Sam. I'll catch up with Sam during tutor time. Sam is a good friend. Sam likes me.	Sam doesn't like me anymore. Sam's avoiding me. I'm not worth knowing. The whole day is ruined. I bet Sam will ignore me during tutorial.
A science lesson doesn't interest you	This lesson isn't very interesting. The next lesson will be better. I usually like science. I'm good at science. Not every lesson can be exciting.	Science is really boring. I hate science. School is a waste of time. I can't do this. I'm no good at science.

Class discussion

Has anyone got an example of permanent or global thinking they would like to share?

How might the thinking be changed in the future to be more optimistic?

When are you most likely to catastrophize and blame yourself generally?

How can you apply optimistic thinking in the next few days?

Becoming an Optimistic Thinker

Remember to use the three different kinds of optimistic thinking:

	Optimistic people			Pessimistic people
T	See events as Temporary (sometimes happens)		**P**	See events as Permanent (always happens)
S	See events as Specific (happened on this occasion)		**G**	See events as Global (always happens)
BB	**B**lame themselves for their **B**ehaviour in this event		**BG**	Blame themselves Generally

Use the following situations and add how optimistic and pessimistic people would think. An example has been done for you.

Event	Optimistic thinking	Pessimistic thinking
You've done a test but don't think it has gone very well.	S - I didn't do very well in that test. I'll do better next time.	G - I flunked as usual. I'm just thick.
You have just fallen out with one of your good friends.		
Your parents are arguing and you think they are going to split up.		
Your pet has died.		
You get into trouble for something you didn't do.		
A teacher shouts at you and you get a detention. You don't think it is fair.		
You get ditched by a mate so that he can be part of a 'cool' group.		

Storyboards for Optimism

When you have written the optimistic and pessimistic thinking in each situation, take one of the scenarios and develop it into a storyboard.

Example:

	TEACHER	STUDENT
THINKING	My lesson is interrupted by Natasha again.	I'll be in trouble for being late. I'm cross with Mrs Price.
FEELING	Frustrated, and cross at the interruption.	Anxious about being late. Indignant about unfairness.
BEHAVING	Gets cross. Unnecessarily accuses Natasha.	Defensive and aggressive. Uses sharp voice.

Work in a small group, make a short play from your storyboard and show it to the rest of the class.

2) Imagination

Adult notes

This section presents some activities that you can do with your class and some that you can give them to do on their own or in pairs. Imagination is like a muscle; it develops and grows stronger when it is used. Sometimes students need permission to use their imagination. They are so used to being asked to produce the 'right answer' in school that they don't feel comfortable with imaginative thinking and lateral ideas. If you can create a classroom climate that encourages unusual and imaginative thinking, the students will soon become familiar with it and spur one another on to greater levels of creativity.

Imaginative metaphors

Use metaphors to develop imagination. Metaphors are when we think of one thing as another. For instance someone once said, 'If I were a vehicle I would be a bright pink Volkswagen beetle because I am bright, cheerful, noticeable and have great curvy lines.'

What would you rather be?

Use the list of metaphors given below and ask the students to stand in one part of the room for the first of the metaphor pairs and in another part of the room for the other.

Once they have chosen their metaphor, ask them to work in pairs or threes and discuss why they chose it. Did other people associate themselves with the metaphor for the same reasons as you or different ones?

Would you rather be:

A lorry or a mini?	**Concrete or wood?**
The sun or the moon?	**A writer or an actor?**
A frog or a snail?	**A hammer or a nail?**
A flower or a tree?	**A tractor or trailer?**
Yes or no?	**Coke or milkshake?**
A circle or a square?	**Foundation or roof?**
Spaghetti or chocolate?	**Pleased or sorry?**

As a whole class, debrief the activity by asking the questions:

How easy was it to decide which metaphor to choose?

How did you feel doing the activity?

What did you discover about yourself and others?

What surprised you?

Quick activities for registration time or as lesson starters

► Create book titles and their authors such as 'Dirty Windows' by Hugh Flundung or 'Low Tide' by Sandy Beach

► Make up the announcements at a posh dinner of funny families such as 'Mr and Mrs Cliff and their son Rocky' or 'Lord and Lady Phant and their daughter Ellie' or 'Mr and Mrs Gator and their son Ali'.

► Imagine you are a famous inventor and describe your latest invention.

Wordsearch for Imagination

J	E	D	P	W	A	C	I	O	N	S	T	C	I	P	S	I	C	E	S
C	U	D	A	F	S	K	N	I	L	E	K	A	M	G	E	S	O	C	S
R	S	G	E	U	W	E	E	O	E	P	A	S	P	N	W	C	L	M	I
E	U	P	R	O	B	L	E	M	S	O	L	V	E	T	O	T	O	N	O
A	A	Z	N	E	N	I	G	Q	U	I	E	I	G	B	N	E	U	P	T
T	O	S	A	D	I	F	F	E	R	E	N	T	S	I	I	N	R	I	S
I	S	S	T	U	C	I	L	H	P	A	T	S	U	P	D	T	S	C	A
V	E	N	I	C	T	D	O	I	E	D	E	T	C	D	E	D	F	I	O
E	F	D	V	N	O	T	S	T	U	C	K	A	C	I	A	K	R	M	E
K	O	T	L	A	S	E	L	B	O	R	P	O	T	F	S	H	X	A	F
L	W	S	P	I	C	R	W	F	V	I	T	S	U	F	O	S	H	G	O
H	O	I	R	C	H	A	R	A	E	R	C	O	N	I	W	D	S	I	O
R	I	M	F	S	Y	X	K	R	Y	L	I	L	U	O	P	T	O	N	L
M	O	A	M	E	T	A	P	H	O	R	S	Y	S	T	I	K	D	A	O
E	S	G	W	A	I	L	I	S	F	D	Y	D	U	S	C	V	I	T	C
T	F	E	R	T	E	H	E	A	U	H	L	E	A	O	T	T	F	I	E
H	O	S	D	R	C	I	S	U	M	O	R	S	L	L	U	W	A	V	S
W	I	K	O	V	L	H	E	Y	R	H	L	L	D	I	R	O	D	E	S
X	K	U	T	S	Y	I	P	O	E	Y	X	H	H	F	E	K	O	N	I
I	M	A	G	I	N	E	S	U	C	C	E	S	S	E	S	E	E	N	K

Words for wordsearch

MAKE LINKS

NOT STUCK

IMAGES

DIFFERENT

COLOUR

IMAGINATIVE

METAPHORS

PICTURES

PROBLEM SOLVE

IDEAS

CREATIVE

UNUSUAL

MUSIC

IMAGINE SUCCESS

Use Your Imagination

Factfile

Eleanor Roosevelt once said, 'The future belongs to those who believe in the beauty of their dreams.'

Imagination is about creating pictures with your thoughts. It involves daydreaming and letting your mind float free. It results in new patterns forming when thoughts link together like when you turn a kaleidoscope and the pieces form a new design.

Imagination is excellent for creative thinking and essential for life in the 21st century.

Sports coaches get athletes to imagine the perfect high jump, the furthest javelin throw, a successful penalty. As they use their imagination, the athletes can see themselves creating the perfect shot or action. Sometimes, they can feel the correct muscles working even though they haven't moved. The result is a much better skill and a far higher success rate.

Your imagination is powerful. Try using it in your revision for the next test that you do.

Try the following with your neighbour…

Think of ten uses for a Wellington boot:

1		6	
2		7	
3		8	
4		9	
5		10	

Think of 5 questions you would like to ask a spoon:

1	
2	
3	
4	
5	

Describe a car for the year 2050

....

....

....

....

3) Integrity

Adult notes

The student handbook gives a page on integrity that contains definitions and a description of what a person with integrity looks like. It is worth remembering that developing integrity in young people involves helping them to know themselves better and encouraging them to be comfortable with who they are. The following activities are about exploring likes and dislikes, beliefs, values and opinions. The worksheets stand alone or they can form the basis of a more extensive discussion. Sometimes individual work is followed by paired or small group work. If you want to, this can be expanded out into whole class discussions for feedback. Discussions can be opened with questions such as:

- ▶ What responses did you give?
- ▶ How did you feel about the responses?
- ▶ What would you like to change in future?
- ▶ What difference will this work on integrity make to you?

Know Yourself

Work on your own to answer the following questions:

1) What is your favourite food?

....

2) Which food do you dislike?

....

3) What TV programme do you enjoy most?

....

4) Which kind of music do you listen to?

....

5) What is your favourite band or artist?

....

6) Which advertisement annoys you most?

....

7) Which is your favourite sport?

....

8) Where have you been on holiday?

....

9) Which part your home town/village/city do you like best?

....

10) Which is your least favourite room in your house and why?

....

11) What is most likely to annoy you?

....

12) Where do you go to find some peace?

....

13) Which subject do you enjoy most?

....

14) Which subject do you enjoy least?

....

15) Which radio station do you listen to?

....

16) What is your favourite film?

....

17) Which part of the day do you like the least?

....

18) If you were the ruler of the land, what law would you pass?

....

19) If you were a great scientist or inventor, what would you like to investigate or make?

....

Join together into groups of two or three and share your answers.
Which one surprised you?
Which one amused you?

Go On, Be Honest!

Work on your own to give yourself a score for how honest you are likely to be in the following situations:

(1 means very unlikely to be honest and 5 means very likely to be honest).

Your mum asks you if you have ever tried smoking.	1	2	3	4	5
You broke a piece of equipment. The teacher asks who did it.	1	2	3	4	5
Person A asked you not to tell something. You told a friend. Person A asks if you told anyone.	1	2	3	4	5
You know who let off the fire alarm. Teachers are asking who did it.	1	2	3	4	5
All your crowd are going to see a film. You don't want to see it but you will be left out.	1	2	3	4	5
Everyone is buying the latest electronic gadget. Your family can't afford to buy it for you.	1	2	3	4	5

Answer the following questions on your own:

I can be honest most easily when...

....

....

I find it really difficult to be honest when...

....

....

I get disappointed with myself when...

....

....

I was most proud of my honesty when..

....

....

Work with a partner and discuss your responses to the questions.

What will you do differently in the future as a result of this work?...

....

....

....

Moral Dilemmas

Choose one of the following moral dilemmas and take five minutes to discuss it with the person next to you. Make a note of your responses and bring your views back to the whole class.

1	What would you do if you found £100 in an envelope on the pavement and nobody saw you pick it up?
2	Is there anything wrong with a 'small' (white) lie to parents or friends to keep from upsetting them?
3	What is your definition of an honest person?
4	It's been said that cheating is just another form of lying. What do you think?
5	What benefits are there in being an honest person?
6	Think of as many excuses as you can for lying. For each one, decide how valid it is.
7	What would you do if a friend of yours gave you an expensive present, then you found out it was stolen?
8	If you tell just one lie, does that make you a liar? How many lies do you have to tell before you are a liar?
9	How do you know if you can trust someone?
10	Do your parents trust you? What could you do that would make your parents stop trusting you?
11	What does trust have to do with honesty?

If there is time, choose another dilemma and do the exercise again.

4) Developing Confidence

Adult notes

In order to grow in confidence people need to develop a better sense of themselves. They need to become attuned to who they are and have a growing sense of what they want to be in life. They also need to become aware of the masks that they wear and the roles that they play. Confidence comes when there is enough self-awareness to be able to make choices about how they are going to present themselves to the outside world and how much they are going to disclose on any occasion. As a teacher, you can help your students to develop their confidence by using a number of different techniques as well as the some of the following student activities.

Drama games for confidence

Alliterative names

Ask the students to stand in a circle and think of their first name. They then think of a positive adjective that starts with the same letter or sound as their name, e.g. 'Cheery Cheryl', 'Jokey Jake', 'Mighty Mary', 'Caring Clarissa' and so on.

Go round the circle and each person introduces themselves using their alliterative name, e.g. 'I am cheery Cheryl'. After each introduction the rest of the group repeats the alliteration by saying, 'You are cheery Cheryl'.

A variation on this activity that requires even more confidence is to get the students to add an action to the alliteration. The individual introduces themselves using the alliterative adjective, their name and the action. The whole group copies the alliteration, name and action back to the individual saying, 'You are...'

Hobbies

Another confidence-building activity is to talk about things we like to do. Ask the students to stand in a circle. Each person thinks of something they like to do outside lessons. They think of an action that represents the chosen activity. Go round the circle and ask each person to say their name followed by their chosen activity. For instance, 'I am Jack and I like playing pool'. The sentence is accompanied by an action to show playing pool. The rest of the circle says, 'Jack plays pool' and copies the action. It is a good idea to ask them to think of different activities that they like doing so that you don't have a class of boys all saying that they like playing football and then taking the opportunity to kick as their chosen action!

Once the names and actions have been learned, everyone in the circle focuses on one person at a time and says the name accompanied by the appropriate action.

Hobby variation

Ask the students to stand or sit in a circle. A volunteer goes into the middle of the circle and performs an action to represent a hobby. Someone from the rest of the class has to guess what the hobby is and everyone in the circle has to copy it.

Talking about confidence

An activity that helps students to increase their self-awareness is to recount actual events to one another in pairs. For instance, pairs could be asked to think of a recent time when they felt they were confident. One person tells the other about an event. The partner has to actively listen without interrupting. They can make encouraging noises such as, 'Oh', 'Mmm, really,' and so on and they can use phrases that reflect some of the content or encourage the other person to continue speaking such as, 'Wow, then what happened?' or, 'Sounds scary,' or, 'Tell me more about...' Once the first person has had a chance to tell their story, the pair swaps round and the other person speaks.

Once this pattern of story telling is established, it can be repeated many times and each time a different aspect of confidence can be highlighted such as 'an occasion when you wish you had been more confident' or 'an occasion when you thought you wouldn't be confident, but turned out to be much bolder than you had expected' and so on. With each of these conversations, the students are encouraged to say what they would do differently next time they found themselves in a similar situation.

Feedback to the whole group

When students work in pairs, it is really helpful to bring some of the learning into the whole group. This is not the time to hear all the stories again, but the pair decides what they will tell the rest of the group that might help the other people to be more self-aware in future. For instance, you could ask the pairs to say something they learned about themselves when they told their story and listened to the other person's story. Or they could report back on something they learned about the other person that they didn't know before. The pairs might report on something they learned about their own level of confidence by listening to another person's story or some advice on ways to be more confident in the future.

Work On Your Confidence

How confident are you in different situations?

Remember: Confidence means being comfortable with yourself. You know what you are like at this stage of your life and accept yourself. It means you are open to new experiences and different ideas.

Work on your own and circle **Y** for yes, you do this and **N** for no, you don't do it.

	YES	NO
Do you often put your hand up to answer questions in class?	Y	N
Have you even taken part in a talent contest?	Y	N
Have you ever asked someone out to their face?	Y	N
Do you own a reptile?	Y	N
Have you been on a big roller coaster?	Y	N
Do you have more than five friends?	Y	N
Have you ever been involved in a physical fight?	Y	N
Have you ever had to stand up and speak in front of the class?	Y	N
Have you ever cried when a teacher told you off?	Y	N
Have you ever been upset when you had a bad test result?	Y	N

Discuss with a partner which of these statements is most likely to show that a person is confident.

Do any of the statements not show confidence?

Bring your feedback to the whole class and see if you agree with the rest of the group.

Self-image and Self-esteem

Confidence is boosted by a positive self-image and healthy self-esteem.

* Self-image is the way you see yourself.

* Self-esteem is the way you value yourself.

* Low self-esteem is created when you don't live up to your expectations or those of other people.

* Get a healthier self-image.

* Learn to see the things in yourself that your best friend sees in you.

* Learn to have realistic expectations.

* Learn to accept imperfections.

* Accept getting things wrong (If we don't make a mistake, we probably won't make anything).

* Focus on your best qualities.

* Believe that you are worth it.

* Be prepared to change.

'The state of your life is nothing more than a reflection of your state of mind.'
Dr Wayne W Dyer

Build Your Self-esteem

Fill in the following statements:

I am good at..

....

My greatest skill is...

....

Something I learned to do recently is...

....

I taught someone how to ....

....

If I am able to I want to ....

....

I am a good friend when ....

....

I have helped others by ....

....

My proudest moment was...

....

An exciting thing I did once was...

....

My scariest moment was ....

....

The best decision I ever made was ....

....

The hardest thing I have ever done is ....

....

Compare your answers with those of a partner then fill in the following statement:

Last week I felt good about myself when...

....

Decide together what you will do to increase your self-esteem during the next week.

'Don't measure yourself by what you have accomplished, but by what you should have accomplished with your ability.' John Wooden

Self-perception and How Others See Me

'Oh the grace that God would gi' us to see ourselves as others see us.'
Robby Burns

Think about the image you have of yourself. Fill in the table below with how you view yourself. Imagine what kind of vehicle or food you would be or which TV or film character you would be.

Fold the page over and ask one or two friends to fill it in about you.

	How I see myself	How .... sees me	How .... sees me
Five or six words that describe you	....	....	....
Vehicle	....	....	....
TV or film character	....	....	....
Food	....	....	....
Musical instrument	....	....	....

Take some time to compare the results and explore how you see yourself and how other people see you.

As a whole class, discuss the exercise. What happened?

Did your friend(s) have a different image of you from the one you had?

What did you learn?

What will you do as a result of your learning?

Be a World-class Adviser

The following short letters have been written to an Agony Aunt in a magazine. Work in pairs and imagine you are the Agony Aunt. It is your job to write an answer to each of the letters. Write your response in the space provided.

Dear Agony Aunt

I have a school play coming up and I feel really scared and am not sure that I can play my part. What can I do to become more confident?

....
....
....

Dear Agony Aunt

There is this really cute boy (or girl) in my class and I really want to ask him (her) out but I am scared. I don't have much confidence. Please help!

....
....
....

Dear Agony Aunt

When we have to work with people who aren't my friends, I get really shy and don't want to say anything. What can I do?

....
....
....

Dear Agony Aunt

I'm always getting into fights at school. I think that people are talking about me behind my back but I can't prove it. Please help me.

....
....
....

Dear Agony Aunt

There is this group of boys who play football at break. I really want to be part of the group, but my football isn't that great. What can I do?

....
....
....

Domain Two – Self-control

DOMAIN TWO
Self-control

5) Using anger well

5) Using anger well

Adult notes

Anger is an emotion that most teenagers have difficulty managing at one time or another. It would be impossible to enumerate all the resources available on anger management. Some that you might find helpful when working with students are listed in the bibliography and you would have to look at them and decide which you prefer (McKay and Maybell, 2004; Faupel et al, 1998; Bohensky, 2001; Fitzell, 2004; Wilde, 1997).

The key to working on anger management is to raise awareness of:

► the range of emotions that come under the umbrella heading of 'anger'

► the general causes and effects of anger

► our own particular anger triggers

► the things that influence how long or short our fuse is

► how to avoid getting angry inappropriately

► how to calm down if we have an angry outburst.

I am not aiming to provide an exhaustive course in anger management in this book. Rather, I suggest that you select some or all of the worksheets that follow as introductions to the ideas. They will help you work with your students as they begin to understand their anger and how to manage it. If you have the time, you could move from this springboard on to more detailed and intensive work on anger management.

The most important thing for you to recognise, as the adult, is that anger is made up of:

► feelings

► thinking

► behaving.

Anger involves every part of us. Acting or behaving in an angry way is the last part of anger. Before we lose our temper or have an angry explosion, we will have had angry thoughts and angry feelings that have built up inside. The main task of anger management is to enable students to recognise the thoughts and feelings and do something about them before they spill over into angry actions.

Recognising What Anger Does to Your Body

Anger affects different people in different ways. Put the labels in the right place on the body outline to see which body parts can be affected.

Clenched fists

Fast heart rate

Quick, shallow breathing

Red face

Tense muscles in face

Adrenalin in whole of body

Tense jaw

Clenched teeth

Tight shoulders and neck

Can't think

Dilated pupils in eyes

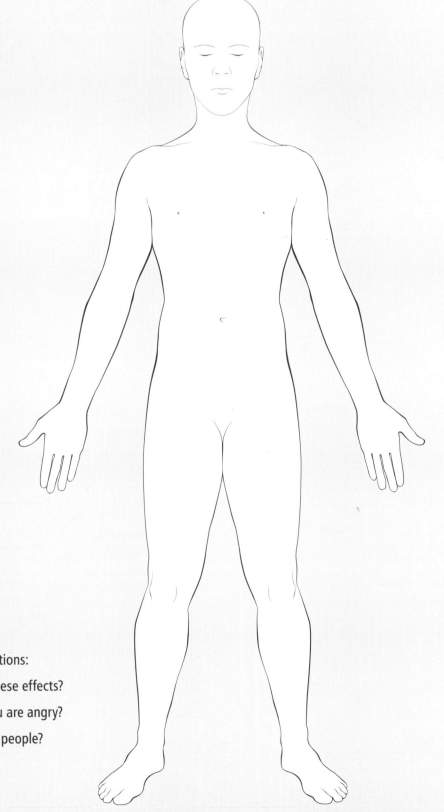

In pairs answer the following questions:

Did anything surprise you about these effects?

Which ones apply to you when you are angry?

Which ones do you notice in other people?

A Model of Anger

Anger is like a firework with three parts.

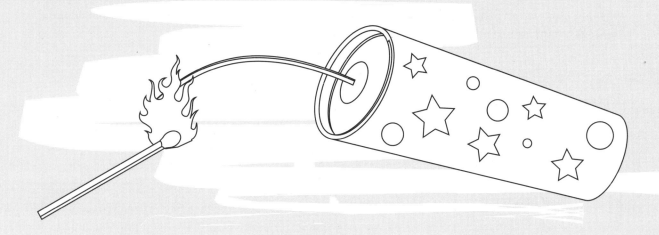

The Match	The Fuse	The Firework
The match sets light to your anger. It could be events such as an unkind comment, someone ignoring you, disrespect for your family, a put down or people laughing at you.	The fuse is the mind reacting. It is the thoughts and feelings which might burn for a short or a long time. Short fuse: Tired, hungry, disappointed, upset, anxious, distracted, afraid, nervous, rushed, agitated, stressed, worried, uneasy, apprehensive. Long fuse: Calm, happy, content, mellow, chilled, fresh, satisfied, at ease, pleased, peaceful, serene, relaxed.	The explosive is the body responding and usually results in anger being expressed. The explosion is recognised by many different responses such as loud voices, swearing, sudden, strong, violent movements, angry tone of voice, shrill voices, a cold response, very controlled movements, ignoring, walking away, damage to property, crying, completely losing control.

Which of These Expressions of Anger do You Recognise in Yourself?

Give each one a score to say if it is not something you do when you are angry (1) or it is something you are very likely to do when you are angry (4).

	Never	Very occasionally	Quite often	Definitely me
Angry responses	1	2	3	4
Loud voice				
Swearing				
Sudden, strong, violent movements				
Angry tone of voice				
Shrill voice				
A cold response				
Very controlled movements				
Ignoring				
Walking away				
Damage to property				
Crying				
Throwing things				
Completely losing control				

In pairs compare your scores with your neighbour.

Talk about when you are likely to show the different angry responses.

When are you unlikely to show how angry you are?

What do you do to try to control your anger?

Matches That Light Our Anger

We all have things that are likely to make us feel angry.

What triggers you?

Tick the things on the list below that are likely to light your anger fuse.

Not getting your own way		Someone taking your things without asking	
Being left out		Someone breaking your things	
Being ignored		Other people getting hurt	
Being called names		Being shouted at	
Being teased		Losing at football	
Someone saying something rude about your family		Being called a liar	
Being told off in front of your friends		Being pushed	
Getting something wrong		People bullying your friends	
Looking stupid		Having to do something you don't want to do	
Being treated unfairly		Being told off and other people are not	
Rules you don't agree with		Being lied to	

Other things that make me angry are:

1)...

2)...

3)...

4)...

Bring the information together by doing a class survey on anger.

What is the most common trigger in your class? ....

Which is the least common trigger in your class? ....

What could you do in the next few days to reduce the number of times people are triggered into anger?

I will reduce anger in our class this week by ....

....

....

....

Think Cool and Lengthen Your Fuse

When your fuse is lit and you start to feel angry you can do two things. You can think hot and pour petrol on your anger so that there is a big explosion, or you can think cool and lengthen the time it takes for you to react and become angry. Sometimes thinking cool means you do not even get really angry.

Katy was called some really unkind names by two friends, Hayley and Tahlee. To start with she could only think that they didn't like her any more and that they were not going to be her friends. She was furious because she couldn't think of any good reason for their unkindness and felt very badly treated. When Katy thought about it some more, she remembered that she had told Josh that Hayley fancied him. She had agreed to go to town with Rosie on Saturday and neither Hayley nor Tahlee liked Rosie.

The Trigger	Hot thoughts	Cool thoughts
Friends call you names.	They don't like me.	They are mad because I told Josh.
	They are so petty.	They are upset that I am being friendly to Rosie.
	I'm not going to be their friend any more.	They are afraid that I will like Rosie more than them.

Cool thoughts make your fuse longer so you are less likely to get angry.

Think Cool

Hot thoughts	Cool thoughts
Come quickly,	Take time,
e.g. thoughts like, 'People are out to get me.'	e.g. thoughts like, 'I wonder why she/he did that?'
'They did it on purpose.'	'I need to find out more about what happened.'

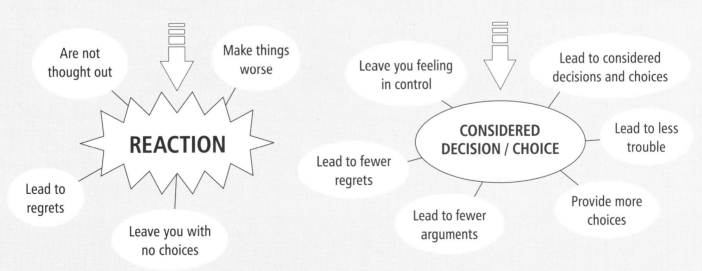

REACTION

Are not thought out

Make things worse

Lead to regrets

Leave you with no choices

CONSIDERED DECISION / CHOICE

Leave you feeling in control

Lead to considered decisions and choices

Lead to less trouble

Lead to fewer regrets

Lead to fewer arguments

Provide more choices

Act first, think later

Act at speed
Regret at leisure

Think first, then act

Decide at leisure
Wiser actions

Think Cool

Identify hot and cool thoughts where H stands for hot, C stands for cool:

Situation	Thoughts	C	H
Someone throws a ball. It hits Sam.	'That was on purpose.'		
	'I'll get him.'		
	'Was that an accident or was it on purpose?'		
	'He'll wish he never messed with me.'		
	'What happened?'		
Tariq is supposed to meet a friend at the end of school. He doesn't turn up.	'What's going on?'		
	'This is a really annoying'		
	'Maybe he got into trouble and was delayed'		
	'He is such a jerk'		
	'He is supposed to be my friend. Some friend!'		
	'I'll call him later and see what happened.'		
	'He's always late.'		

Catch What You Think

Work on your own to fill in the hot thoughts people are likely to have in the following situations then change them to cool thoughts. The first one has been done for you.

Trigger	Hot thoughts	Cool thoughts
Someone takes your favourite ruler and breaks it.	'He broke that on purpose.' 'I'll break his pen because he broke my ruler.'	'I wonder what happened?' 'Was that an accident or deliberate?'
The teacher shouts at you because you are late to a lesson.		
Someone pushes you over in the corridor.		
Your best friend doesn't talk to you.		
Someone insults your friend.		
A teacher doesn't listen when you try to explain about forgetting the homework.		

In pairs, compare your hot thoughts and cool thoughts.

What similarities and differences do you find in the way you respond to the situations?...............................

....

....

What will you do in the next week to think less hot thoughts and more cool thoughts? ....

....

....

Putting the Match Out

Here are some things people use to calm themselves when they start to feel angry.

On your own, tick any of the ones you have tried.

Talk to a friend you can trust		Take some space, move away from the cause of your anger	
Count to 10		Draw a picture of your anger	
Hit a ball		Play a video game	
Beat a pillow (the pillow can't get hurt)		Run around a field as fast as you can	
Play calming music		Sing along with the stereo	
Go to your room and think cool thoughts		Talk to yourself	
Relax tense muscles		Think about nice things (maybe about a fun holiday or your favourite sport)	
Take a bike ride		Recycle glass bottles (the smashing sounds are soothing)	

Other things I do to help me to stay calm are ....
....
....

In future I will try..
....
....

Share your findings with a friend.

Using Anger Well

Once you have developed some ways of avoiding an angry explosion, the next challenge is to use your anger effectively by learning how to express your anger in a way that respects the other person's feelings and point of view.

When you use anger well you can:

* **disagree with someone respectfully**

* **resolve conflicts**

* **sort out misunderstandings**

* **develop better relationships.**

Rules of expressing anger well:

Do:

- wait until you are calm
- clearly say how you feel
- be accurate about what actually happened
- respect the other person's point of view even if you don't agree with it
- offer a way forward so that it can be done differently next time.

Don't:

- blame the other person
- put the other person down
- become aggressive
- exaggerate what happened.

The Alphabet of Anger Expression

A Say clearly what happened

B Say how it made you feel (Talk about what happened using 'I')

C Say the effect it had on you or what you did

D Say how you would like it to be in the future

Example:

A When people call me names

B I feel hurt and angry.

C Then I call them names back and don't want to talk to them.

D I would like us to stop calling one another names.

The alphabet of appropriate anger is called an 'I' message because we are speaking for ourselves and not blaming others.

Example:

'You' message (blames the other person)		'I' message (speak for yourself and use the alphabet)
You are always borrowing my equipment and then losing it. Why can't you get your own stuff?	**A**	When people borrow my equipment and lose it.
	B	I feel frustrated and angry.
	C	I don't have equipment for my lessons and have to keep buying new stuff.
	D	I would like you to get some equipment of your own.

The Alphabet of Anger Expression (cont.)

Try your own 'I' messages using the alphabet of appropriate anger for the following situations.

Being pushed out of the front of the queue for lunch

'You' message (blames the other person)	'I' message (speak for yourself and use the alphabet)
....	....

Being accused of deliberately not doing your homework

'You' message (blames the other person)	'I' message (speak for yourself and use the alphabet)
....	....

Being shouted at for being late to a lesson

'You' message (blames the other person)	'I' message (speak for yourself and use the alphabet)
....	....

If you have time, work in pairs and think of other times when 'you' messages are used. Write the 'you' message in the space below. ....

....

Turn the 'you' message into an 'I' message...

....

Domain Three – Understanding Others

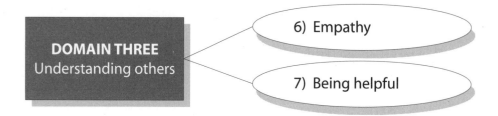

6) Empathy

Adult notes

Developing empathy in young people is done by providing opportunities for them to see things from someone else's point of view. This is work that lends itself to writing scripts for different people and then role playing the different characters in given scenarios.

Empathy Ratings

Empathy is the ability to identify with another person's feelings.

Empathy is the ability to see and feel things as others see and feel them.

There is an old North American Indian saying which asks us never to judge another person until we have walked a mile in his moccasins.

People who are good at empathy have the following qualities and skills. Rate yourself to see how strong you would be.

Empathy Skills	Rate how much this is like you, 0 (not at all like me) to 10 (this is really like me)
Listening – I can give my full attention when listening to someone else	
Point of view – I can recognise when someone else does not think the same way as I do	
Feelings – I can recognise how people are feeling when they tell me things	
Judgement – I can stop myself from jumping to conclusions	
Open-minded – I can remain open-minded so that I can hear different points of view	
Flexible – I can swap sides of the argument to see things from each point of view	
Enjoy differences – I can understand different opinions from my own	

A time when I showed empathy in the last week was...

....

....

A time when I wish other people had shown more empathy in the last week was.................................

....

....

In pairs compare your results.

Write down one person you know who is good at empathising (adult or child) ....

....

ACTIVITY SHEET

Empathy Lenses

How good are you at seeing in different colours?

Empathy is like wearing glasses with different coloured lenses. Each colour represents a different person's point of view. Empathy is about recognising what someone else may be thinking and feeling.

In pairs take it in turns to put on the different coloured lenses for each of the people in the following scenarios. Each person in the pair chooses a character from the scenario.

Speak for your character, saying what they are thinking and what they are feeling. Swap round so that you take the view of the other character. Write down the thinking and feeling that you discover.

 In the games lesson, two team leaders are chosen. They have to pick their teams for the game. Rashid is not picked for either of the teams.

Character	Thinking	Feeling
Rashid		
Team leaders		

 Sherrie is allowed to go to a friend's house until 9pm. She doesn't get home until 10.30

Character	Thinking	Feeling
Sherrie		
Her parents		

 In a science lesson, some chemical is spilt. Nathan was messing around as usual and the teacher assumed he had knocked the beaker over. Nathan was told off, but he hadn't done it, Josh had.

Character	Thinking	Feeling
Teacher		
Nathan		

Flexibility – Which Side of the Argument Are You On?

Decide whether you agree or disagree with these statements.

	Agree	Disagree
Cosmetics should be tested on animals		
Fox hunting should be allowed		
Murderers should be executed		
Parents should be allowed to smack their children		
People should be allowed to choose when they die		
Children should be paid to go to school		

In pairs, choose a statement. (You can choose one where you have different points of view, or take opposite sides of the argument no matter what you really think.)

One of you is to argue for the statement and the other argues against it.

The person who argues for the statement speaks first and has one minute to present their argument.

The person who argues against the statement may not interrupt, but must listen carefully.

After a minute the person who argues against the statement may speak for a minute.

When you have finished, swap round and see if you can speak for the opposite point of view.

Reflection in the whole group

What happened during the exercise?

How easy was it to hear the other person's point of view?

What did you find out about the way you think and feel?

How will you apply your learning in the future?

Role-plays for Empathy

Taking part in a role play is a really good way to develop your empathy. Remember to show Thoughts and Feelings. In groups of three try these scenarios.

Brought home by the police

The police have just brought a young person home to her parents. Decide what the problem was and how you will show each of the points of view.

	Thoughts	Feelings
Police	....	....
Young person	....	....
Parent	....	....

Called in to school

A teacher calls a parent into school to talk about his child's behaviour. Decide what has happened and show each of the points of view in your drama.

	Thoughts	Feelings
Parent	....	....
Student	....	....
Teacher	....	....

Bully and victim

A mediator has set up a meeting to help both parties understand what has happened. Decide what has taken place and how you will represent each of the points of view.

	Thoughts	Feelings
Bully	....	....
Victim	....	....
Mediator	....	....

Over to You

Choose three situations where empathy would help.

	Situation	How empathy helps
1		
2		
3		

Draw storyboards or comic strips to show your situation. Use speech bubbles to show how the different people think and feel.

7) Being helpful

Adult notes

Being helpful is an extension of empathy. It is the action someone would take in response to feeling empathic. The following activities are ways of focusing students' attention on the things they can do to show that they understand someone else's situation. It is important to remember that being empathic does not always mean that we have to do something about it however. We can demonstrate our understanding of someone else's situation by listening to them. Sometimes it is appropriate to actively respond to the things that we hear. Encourage students to think about when it is appropriate to do something and when listening is enough.

What Would You Do?

In each of the following situations, see if you can think of three things you might do in order to improve the situation and make the other person feel better.

Situation		What you do		
1	Your mum has loads of housework to do. She is feeling stressed.	**1**	....	
		2	....	
		3	....	
2	A friend has been ditched by his girlfriend. He is feeling sad.	**1**	....	
		2	....	
		3	....	
3	Your older brother or sister has exams. They are feeling frustrated with revising.	**1**	....	
		2	....	
		3	....	

What Would You Do? (cont.)

	Situation		What you do
4	Your tutor has too many things to do in tutor time. She seems to be in a bad mood.	1 2 3	
5	A friend hasn't been invited to a party lots of people are going to. He is feeling left out.	1 2 3	
6	Someone in your science group doesn't understand the work. She feels stupid.	1 2 3	

Problem-solving Using Imagination, Empathy and Cool Thinking

The four steps to solving problems

1) Stop and think – slow down (use your self-control).
2) Look at the problem from the other person's point of view (use your empathy).
3) Go for a solution – choose a solution and make a list of possible ways of getting there (use your imagination).
4) How did it go? If the solution didn't work, try another.

Example

You want to go to a friend's party. It doesn't finish until 11.30pm and you usually have to be in by 9.30. Your mum won't let you go.

Step 1

Stop and think – change your hot thoughts for cool ones

Most people react strongly when they are not allowed to do what they want to do. Try changing your hot thoughts into cool ones.

Hot thoughts	Cool thoughts
She is so mean	She cares about me
She always spoils my fun	She is worried about my safety
Other mums are much more easy going	She doesn't know if there will be alcohol or drugs
She's a killjoy	She doesn't know how I'm going to get home
Everyone else is going	Maybe some other people won't be allowed to go

Step 2

Look at the problem from the other person's point of view

Use your cool thoughts to think how your mum is feeling. She is concerned that you will be out late with no way of getting home safely. She loves you and wants to make sure that you stay safe and she doesn't know what will go on at the party. She wants you to have enough sleep at night so that you don't sleep all the next day. Maybe she is particularly concerned if you are planning to go out on a school night.

Step 3

Go for a solution or goal

Different people might have different goals in any scenario. If your goal is that you want your friends to accept you but you don't want to upset your mum, how are you going to make it happen?

Remember to take into account the other person's point of view. You could offer to:

- Arrange for an adult that your mum trusts to bring you home promptly at 11.30.
- Make sure your mum knows the party is on Saturday night.
- Ask your mum to ring your friend's parents so that she knows the party will be safe and supervised.

Step 4

How did it go?

If the plan was successful then all is well. If it still doesn't work and your mum still won't let you go to the party, then rethink. Set a new goal such as, 'I won't go to this party, but I'll see if I can have a party at my house soon so my mum can supervise it.'

Go through steps two, three and four with each solution until you come up with one that works for you.

Try your Own Problem-solving

Use the following scenarios to try out your problem-solving skills.

For each one, work on your own to fill in steps 1, 2, 3 and 4.

	You get a test back and the teacher has added up the score wrongly. You have a lower mark than you should have.
Step 1	....
Step 2	....
Step 3	....
Step 4	....

	Your parents are going out for the evening and have said that you can have one friend over. You want to invite three friends and want them to leave early so that you can clear up before your parents get home.
Step 1	....
Step 2	....
Step 3	....
Step 4	....

Try your Own Problem-solving (cont.)

You go to town to buy a birthday present for your friend. While you are there you see a CD that you really want. You haven't enough money to buy both the CD and your friend's present.	
Step 1	....
Step 2	....
Step 3	....
Step 4	....

Choose one of the scenarios and work with some other people to role-play your solution and see if it works.	
Step 1	....
Step 2	....
Step 3	....
Step 4	....

Domain Four – Getting On With Others

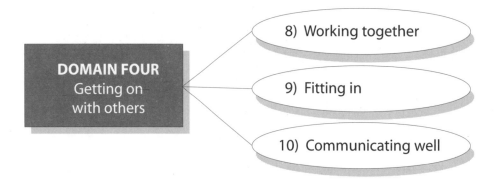

8) Working Together

Adult notes

Students recognise that an ability to work in a group situation is essential to being able to do well at school. Yet secondary schools often give little or no time to developing the skills and qualities that are needed for an individual to work productively in a group. The school places students in many different groups: tutor groups, teaching groups, year groups, small working groups, teams and so on and seems to assume that they will be able to work together without any additional support or training.

The idea that we can put thirty or so young people in the same room and expect them to be able to work as a group, or even as a number of smaller groups is questionable, from both a theoretical and an experiential point of view. As teachers we can probably all recall times when we have put students into groups of four or five and though they sat at the same cluster of tables and took part in the same task, little or no interaction took place between the group members. The students in my research indicated that what happens is that the more vocal students take over. They organise the others with varying degrees of success and then everyone works independently on their bit of the task before bringing it together at the end. In a less productive context, the students said that some people disrupt the work other people are trying to do and some become overtly angry, making it impossible for the group to complete the task.

Experiences like these illustrate the fact that effective groups do not just happen. For adults to expect a disparate and assorted set of individuals to work together productively in the pursuit of a common goal is unrealistic. The ability to work together effectively develops when teachers work in a way that enables their students to acquire the knowledge and skills of participation. The teacher has to intervene to promote group development. As teachers we may need continuing professional development in understanding and developing effective groups. Even when we feel competent to build the skills and conditions that encourage people to work well together, group formation can still be difficult as it is often neither linear nor straightforward. Sometimes there are periods of tiny, barely perceptible improvements and then there may be a 'growth spurt' and a great leap forward accompanied by the almost tangible benefits of greater cohesion and more supportive relationships.

Working in Teams

Teams work when people take on different roles. These include people who:

*contribute
have ideas and make suggestions

*organise
keep everyone on task, make sure the task is clear and keep time

*encourage
listen to everyone and make sure all ideas are heard

*make connections
notice how ideas fit together and, build on ideas.

In groups of five, one person is the observer and fills in the observation sheet noting the contributions that each person makes.

The other four deal out a pack of cards between them. The task is to make a house of cards with everyone taking part and contributing cards for the house. The time limit is five minutes.

Working in Teams Observation Sheet

Group name:				
Group roles	Name 1	Name 2	Name 3	Name 4
Contributing **Making suggestions** **Having ideas**				
Organising **Making sure task is clear** **Making sure task is done** **Keeping time**				
Encouraging **Listening** **Making sure everyone is heard**				
Making connections **Noticing links between ideas** **Building on ideas**				

Debrief the experience in your group of four before you get feedback from the observer.

• How did you get on?

• What went well?

• Who took on which roles?

After the observer has given the feedback discuss the following questions:

• What surprised you about the feedback?

• What have you learned?

• What will you do next time?

Repeat the activity and ask someone else to be the observer.

Group Characters

Every group has a whole variety of characters. Some are helpful, some are not. Here are some characters you might recognise. Sort them into helpful and unhelpful to the group.

For the unhelpful ones, say what the individual character might do to improve the way the group works.

Say what the group as a whole might do to make the group work better. The first character has been done for you.

Character	Helpful/ Unhelpful	What character does	How individual might change	How group might deal with character
Mouse	Unhelpful	Is silent and is too shy to contribute	Take a risk and try to be bolder	Allow time for the 'mouse' to have a say or ask the 'mouse' to write down his or her ideas
Time keeper				
Irritator				
Ideas person				
Finisher				
Loud mouth				
Doer				
Organiser				
Peace keeper				
Co-ordinator				
Joker				
Decision maker				
Leader				

9) Fitting In

Adult notes

Finding a way to fit into the peer group is probably the single most challenging task of adolescence. In school there is a jostling mass of young people all trying to find a place and make their mark. They want to assert their individuality enough to be recognised in the crowd. Yet they don't want to be ostracised for being weird, so they have to conform enough to blend into the group. Fitting in is about finding points of connection without losing individuality. It is a fine balance between accommodation and assertion. Many young people find themselves being overly passive in order to be accommodating or overly aggressive in order to assert themselves. Students in the study recognised the need to find a good middle path so that they could be part of the group but not 'taken over' by it. They also recognised a need to be apart from the group with personal integrity and individuality, without alienating the rest of their team. As students talk about these different aspects of fitting in, so they develop the skills and confidence to find a good middle path that honours their individuality and respects the peer group.

Fitting In Wordsearch

T	O	C	O	W	E	N	I	G	R	E	S	E	C	O	R	T
S	F	I	T	I	N	S	N	O	C	X	E	W	O	B	E	H
D	I	C	H	T	R	I	E	W	A	I	L	O	N	E	R	O
O	T	T	G	H	S	G	N	I	N	B	F	J	S	O	Y	U
M	P	R	O	M	U	O	H	T	Z	Y	I	Q	I	F	E	G
I	S	E	L	F	I	S	H	H	T	F	N	R	P	L	S	H
N	C	R	D	E	Y	T	I	F	E	P	D	T	Z	E	E	E
A	O	P	N	O	R	H	N	L	P	L	J	F	Q	X	L	S
T	N	S	I	D	E	O	D	O	V	E	R	I	T	I	F	B
E	S	P	Y	I	E	J	E	W	E	Q	B	S	I	B	L	E
L	I	R	E	S	P	E	C	T	F	U	L	H	O	L	O	G
B	D	E	T	R	O	J	Y	P	L	Y	E	S	B	E	B	O
Z	E	R	C	A	R	I	N	G	I	Q	L	J	A	I	L	Y
B	R	G	O	C	O	Z	T	H	O	U	G	H	T	F	U	L
C	A	R	M	S	M	E	Q	I	R	W	J	Z	E	T	I	R
J	T	R	E	S	O	L	V	E	C	O	N	F	L	I	C	T
N	E	I	O	L	F	L	E	X	K	T	L	O	K	I	T	A
I	X	T	A	K	E	O	V	E	R	A	T	F	I	T	I	K
K	C	O	M	P	R	O	M	I	S	E	T	L	N	O	B	E
P	R	B	V	L	O	S	E	E	I	B	L	E	D	E	Y	O

Words for wordsearch

SELFISH	RESOLVE CONFLICT
DOMINATE	COMPROMISE
FIT IN	CONSIDERATE
GO WITH FLOW	CARING
TAKE OVER	KIND
LONER	THOUGHTFUL
FLEXIBLE	RESPECTFUL

Work Out How Well You Fit In

Start here and follow the arrows:

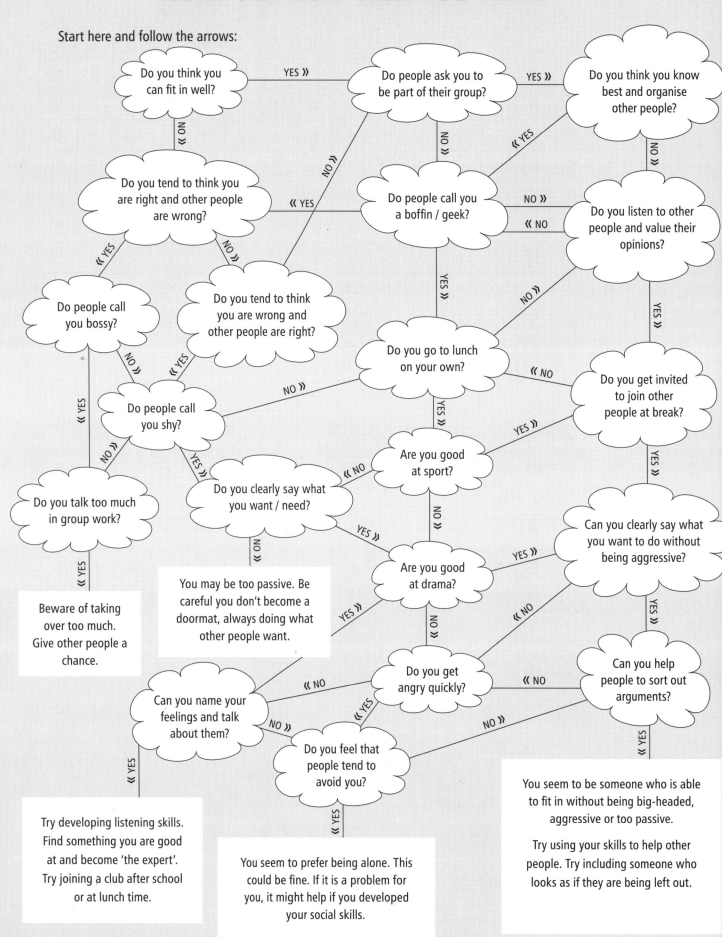

Do you think you can fit in well?

YES ≫

Do people ask you to be part of their group?

YES ≫

Do you think you know best and organise other people?

NO ≪

Do you tend to think you are right and other people are wrong?

≪ YES

Do people call you a boffin / geek?

≪ YES

NO ≪

NO ≫

NO ≫ / ≪ NO

Do you listen to other people and value their opinions?

≪ YES

Do people call you bossy?

NO ≫

Do you tend to think you are wrong and other people are right?

≪ YES

YES ≫

Do you go to lunch on your own?

NO ≫

≪ NO

YES ≫

Do you get invited to join other people at break?

≪ YES

Do people call you shy?

YES ≫

NO ≫

YES ≫

Do you talk too much in group work?

YES ≫

Do you clearly say what you want / need?

NO ≪

Are you good at sport?

YES ≫

NO ≫

Can you clearly say what you want to do without being aggressive?

YES ≫

NO ≫

YES ≫

Are you good at drama?

YES ≫

NO ≫

Beware of taking over too much. Give other people a chance.

You may be too passive. Be careful you don't become a doormat, always doing what other people want.

Can you name your feelings and talk about them?

≪ NO

Do you get angry quickly?

≪ NO

Can you help people to sort out arguments?

≪ YES

NO ≫

≪ YES

Do you feel that people tend to avoid you?

NO ≫

YES ≪

Try developing listening skills. Find something you are good at and become 'the expert'. Try joining a club after school or at lunch time.

You seem to prefer being alone. This could be fine. If it is a problem for you, it might help if you developed your social skills.

You seem to be someone who is able to fit in without being big-headed, aggressive or too passive.

Try using your skills to help other people. Try including someone who looks as if they are being left out.

Fitting In with Integrity – Finding the Middle Path

Not a doormat, that is, completely passive.

Not a bully, that is, overly aggressive.

Find the middle road of assertiveness.

Four steps to assertiveness:

1) Describe the situation that is upsetting you – without heat, without blame, without interpreting causes.

2) Say how you feel – clearly and without blame.

3) Say what you want the other person to change – clearly, with specific detail.

4) Say how the change would make you feel.

The Art of Sharing

Sharing means letting other people use your ideas, equipment and talent.

How well do you share?

How do other people see you? Ask a friend, a teacher and a family member to fill in the form.

(10 very likely to see this quality in me, 1 very unlikely to see this quality in me)

Sharing Quality	Friend	Teacher	Family	How I see myself
Generous				
Lend equipment				
Return borrowed things				
Contribute good ideas				
Look after other people's things				
Break other people's things				
Selfish				
Take the best for yourself				
Think about other people				

Discuss the findings of your table with a friend.

Does everyone see you as equally able to share?

Who sees you as most able to share?

What qualities do you think they see?

What could you do to improve your ability to share?

What would you need from other people in order to be able to share more freely?

Whole group

Take feedback in the whole group about ways of increasing the amount of sharing. Decide on an action plan to enable each person in the group to share more freely.

10) Communicating Well

Adult notes

The main skills of communication are speaking and listening. These are skills that are developed in the English and drama curricula and with every foreign language. In fact, every teacher in every classroom works hard to ensure that students speak appropriately, in turn and that they listen to each other. Yet we still have difficulty with these important skills, often into adult life.

The students recognised that communicating well is one of the most important skills for doing well in school. When young people can't listen to others or wait their turn to speak, the classroom becomes a disorganised and difficult place where a few louder voices dominate and many quieter voices are never heard. As I listened to the young people's view, it became clear that speaking was not the major problem. Even very quiet or shy students could be encouraged to speak if the listening climate was good enough. The major problem was listening. Students were reluctant to put their own views to one side long enough to hear someone else's; they wanted to be heard but not to hear. Teachers and other adults working with young people can play an important role in helping them to do well at school by teaching the skills of active listening and by modelling excellent listening when they deal with young people.

Whole Body Listening

'I think I learn more from listening. Anything I would say I already know.' Anonymous

Work in pairs

In each pair one person is A and the other B.

A tells B about something that interests them (a hobby, a holiday, something they did at the weekend).

B has to show A that he is not listening (this can be by walking away, not looking at the other person, fiddling with things on the desk, talking to someone else and so on).

Swap round so that both feel what it is like not to be listened to.

Debrief

What did it feel like when your partner didn't listen to you?

Repeat the exercise, but this time, listen really carefully.

A speaks about something that interests them and B really listens.

Swap round so that B speaks and A listens.

How did you feel when someone really listened carefully?

How did you know the other person was listening?

Listening or Not Listening

Use the exercises to fill in the table below.

Things people do when they are not listening	Things people do when they are listening
Verbal (Example: Talk to other people)	Verbal (Example: Ask good questions)
....	....
....	....
....	....
....	....
....	....
....	....
....	....
Non-verbal (Example: Turn away from you)	Non-verbal (Example: Turn towards you)
....	....
....	....
....	....
....	....
....	....
....	....
....	....

Complete the following sentences:

A person I find it hard to listen to is...

....

....

I find it hard to listen when I'm...

....

....

I will listen better in the future by..

....

....

Hitting the Jackpot – Listening Accurately

Hearing and listening are two different things.

> 'My friend says I never listen. At least I think that's what he said,' Anonymous

Hearing involves noticing the sounds. Listening involves whole-body focussed attention on the speaker and their words.

Imagine listening like scoring a bull's-eye. Aiming at the bull's-eye is done by listening to your partner and then summarising what they have said to you.

Score 1 – Misunderstanding or misinterpreting what was said.

Score 2 – Missing out some important points or some details.

Score 3 – Feeding back accurately and fully what was said.

Score 4 – Getting behind the words to the 'hidden' message.

Feedback Model

For example: Razor is telling his friend Jordan a story.

Razor says: 'Last week on Tuesday I was supposed to meet my friend Greg to go to town after school. We agreed to meet and when I got there, he was nowhere to be seen so I got mad and went home on my own. Then he rang me up and was mad with me because I wasn't at the meeting place.'

Hitting the Jackpot –
Listening Accurately (cont.)

Score of two

Jordan summarises: 'Last week you were supposed to meet Greg. He didn't turn up so you were angry with him.' This would score 'two' because it misses some of the important points.

Score of three

Jordan summarises: 'Last Tuesday you agreed to meet Greg after school so that you could go into town together. You didn't see him at the agreed meeting place and this made you angry so you went home without him. He rang you up later and was equally mad with you for not turning up either.' This response would score three because it is an accurate summary of what Razor said and is likely to start Razor talking again. He might well say something like, 'Exactly! Anyway, Greg says that he had been at the meeting place and I didn't turn up ...'

Score of four

Jordan summarises: 'Last Tuesday there was a misunderstanding between you and Greg that caused you both to be angry. You had agreed to meet after school to go into town but neither of you could find the other at the agreed meeting place.'

This response could be a score of 'four' and could provide insights for Razor on the situation because he hadn't recognised that the anger was due to a misunderstanding. On the other hand, Razor might say, 'No, there was no misunderstanding, Greg just didn't turn up. He was kept back by a teacher and arrived 20 minutes later' in which case Jordan's attempt at a 'four' was actually a 'one' response.

In groups of three

Give yourselves a letter: A, B or C.

A speaks about a subject that interests her. B listens and reflects what she hears. C observes.

Every time B reflects back what she hears, C gives a score for the listening.

The scores can be one, two, three or four.

At the end of a few minutes, A gives feedback to B about how well he listened. Then C gives feedback on what she observed.

Swap round until everyone has had a turn.

Debrief

How many times did you score a one, two or three?

Did anyone score a bull's-eye four?

What have you learned about your own listening skills?

How will you listen better in the future?

(Activity taken from Mann, T. Creative Thinking Skills)

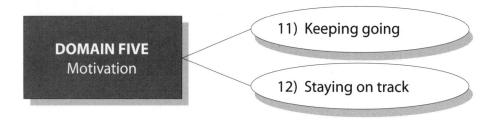

11) Keeping going

Adult notes

Finding ways of encouraging students to remain focussed and motivated are essential to enabling them to get the best out of school. The most important factor in motivation from the student's point of view seems to be a sense of agency in their own learning. They lose motivation when they become overwhelmed by too much work or too hard a task or if they can't see the point of the information they are being asked to learn. A sense of agency can be fostered by talking about how to plan and organise work, how to manage time effectively and how to aim at short and longer term goals. Some schools have experimented with more radical approaches, such as negotiating the content of a topic with the students and pooling knowledge they already have. The teachers found that at the end of the topic, the national curriculum content had been covered, despite approaching the subject as a facilitator of young people's curiosity rather than didactic purveyor of knowledge. It is certainly true that if the students are engaged, can see the relevance and have a goal in sight, they see more point in doing the school work and are better motivated to keep going when the going gets tough. The games and activities found in this section were provided by students from a middle school.

The Power of the Will

Psychologists tell us that motivation, to keep going, needs three things to work together.

Your mind

It is like a computer, storing, coding, processing, retrieving and linking information. It asks the question, 'What?' (For example, 'What happened? What does this mean?')

Your Emotions

They give you feelings about information, or knowledge such as excitement, frustration, anxiety, sadness, happiness, calmness, agitation, boredem or interest. They ask the question 'How do I feel about this learning?'

A Sense of Purpose

It is how you connect what you are learning and how you feel to what you will do. It asks the question, 'Why?' Your sense of purpose gives you the choice about what to do.

You have to manage all three in order to stay motivated with your work.

Opting In and Opting Out

Fill in the table below with your thinking, feeling and choices in two lessons.

Lesson	What do you think?	How do you feel?	What do you do? What choices do you make?
A lesson you really enjoy			
A lesson you don't enjoy			

Discuss in pairs

What could you do to help you to keep going in lessons you don't really like?

Write down four strategies to help you make good choices in lessons that you don't like.

1)...

....

2)...

....

3)...

....

4)...

....

Managing the Feelings

Think of your favourite subject. Imagine you are in the lesson and mark how you usually feel on the scales below:

1	angry	frustrated	agitated	anxious	OK	cool	calm	serene
2	despair	depression	fed up	OK	good	very good	happy	very happy

Think of your least favourite lesson. Imagine you are in the lesson and mark how you usually feel on the scales:

1	angry	frustrated	agitated	anxious	OK	cool	calm	serene
2	despair	depression	fed up	OK	good	very good	happy	very happy

Moving your score up the scale by managing your mood

Did you know that if you change your facial expression you can change your mood?

Try it.

Smile and see how you feel.

Make your face worried and check how you feel.

Frown and describe your feelings.

Did you also know that your body posture affects your mood?

* Try putting your body in a depressed heap and then smile broadly. What happens to your body?

* In pairs, show different moods by your body posture. The other person has to guess your mood by 'reading' your body.

* What could you do differently next time you are in your least favourite lesson to ensure that you are at least in an OK mood and perhaps feel better?

1)..

....

2)..

....

3)..

....

Going for Goals

'If you aim at nothing, you are bound to hit it'

Motivated people have a goal that they are aiming at.

Kelly Holmes won two gold medals in the 2004 Olympics for the 800m and 1500m races. She started running at school and despite several set-backs (including a stress fracture that put her out of the finalists in the 1996 Olympics) she did it.

> **'You need to train hard and be dedicated in what you are trying to achieve. But remember to enjoy what you do.' Kelly Holmes**

What are Kelly's secrets?

* Having a goal
* Believing she could achieve it
* Having a plan and working very hard to achieve it.

On your own

Write down one of your goals ....
....
....

Write down three things you will do to make sure you achieve your goal

1)...

2)...

3..

What is the first step you will take? ....
....
....

'Even the highest mountain in the world is climbed one step at a time.'

12. Staying On Track

Adult notes

The ability to stay on track with the school rules and codes of behaviour can prove the most taxing part of school to some young people. It is not only students who find school work difficult that challenge the rules and codes. There can be students from every ability group and all social classes who find it difficult to behave in an appropriate way. Indeed, most of us will break rules at some time or other if we don't see the reason for the rule or if other circumstances overwhelm our motivation to stay on track. The students in the study appreciated the opportunity to talk about school rules and routines. They found it helpful to examine the conditions that facilitated them keeping to the school rules and the situations when they found themselves breaking rules. This is a sensitive topic and it is important that the students feel safe to look at their behaviour honestly without being afraid that consequences will arise from the discussion. They do need to know that breaking rules does bear consequences in real life, however, so it might help to use some techniques that enable students to look at the issues from a distance without having to talk about themselves.

Staying Focussed

Follow the choices to see how focussed you are likely to be. Which track are you on?

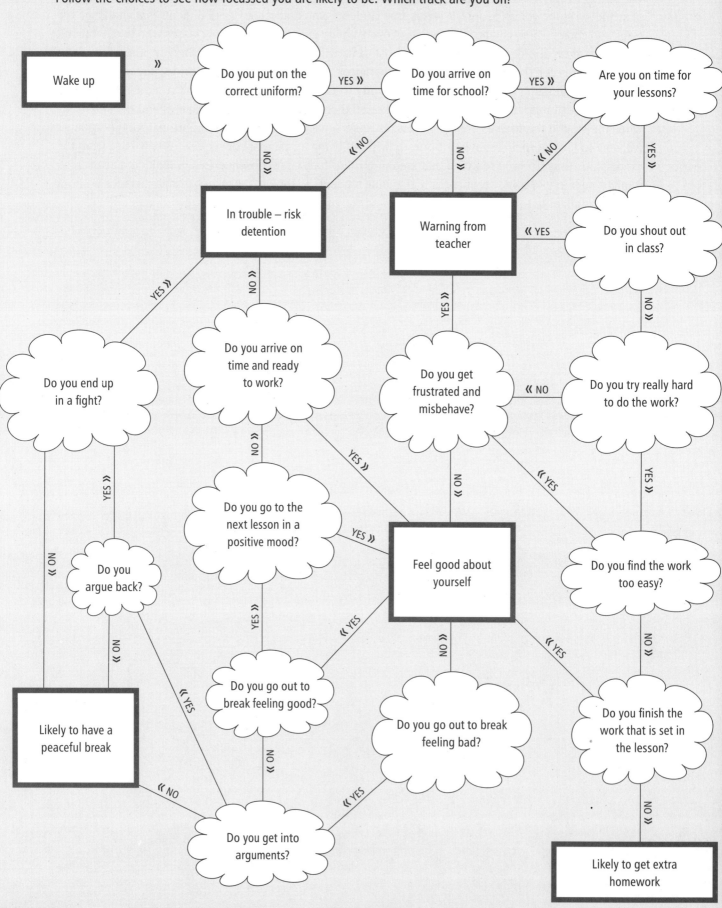

What Would You Do?

The teacher is late for the lesson. The class are waiting outside the door and everyone is getting bored. Someone at the back starts to push the queue. The person behind you falls against you and you lose your balance.

Give four things that might happen:

1)..

2)..

3)..

4)..

For each of the events give the result for you and for other people.

Which would be your preferred outcome for this situation?

Your friend has started to smoke. She has asthma and you are very worried about her. She wants you to try too and is offering to give you a cigarette at break time behind the art block with her new friends.

Give four ways in which you might deal with this situation:

1)..

2)..

3)..

4)..

For each way of dealing with it, give the possible result for you and for other people.

Which option would you choose if this should happen to you?...

Your friend wants you to meet him in the toilets during lesson two. He says that you should both say you need the toilet at 10.15 and then meet up and skive the lesson to have a smoke.

Give four choices you could make:

1)..

2)..

3)..

4)..

What are the consequences of each of your choices for you and for other people?

What option would you choose?...

Summary

In this section you learned how to develop:

► optimisim

► imagination

► integrity

► confidence

► using anger well

► empathy

► being helpful

► working together

► fitting in

► communicating well

► keeping going

► staying on track

by reading notes to adults for working with students and being provided with a range of student activities.

Section Five

The TalkiT Light Edition (TalkiT-LE) Software

In this section you will:

- ▶ be introduced to the TalkiT Light Edition (TalkiT-LE) software that accompanies this book
- ▶ find out how to load and use the software
- ▶ look at the TalkiT-LE questionnaire and the scoring method used
- ▶ learn how to read and use the graphs provided by the TalkiT-LE software
- ▶ consider issues of confidentiality
- ▶ think about how to use the TalkiT-LE profile as an assessment for learning in personal and social education
- ▶ be introduced to the full version of TalkiT.

The TalkiT-LE CD that accompanies this book contains a piece of software that you can either use on a stand alone PC or you can load onto the server in your school so that it is accessible to a class of 30 students. The software is a trial version of TalkiT and comes with enough profiles for 30 students to complete their own self-report questionnaire and for up to five other people to fill in the questionnaire for each individual.

This section explains the:

- ▶ features and functions of TalkiT-LE
- ▶ additional features that are available with the full TalkiT programme.

Getting started with TalkiT-LE

The instructions for installing and using TalkiT-LE are found in the help files on the CD-ROM. I have included a brief synopsis here to help you use the software without any difficulty.

When you put the CD-ROM into the CD driver of your PC or onto the server in the school, the programme will automatically install unless you have turned the automatic loading facility off. You then follow the screens accepting the default options. Once the programme is installed, you go to the start menu, find TalkiT LE and open it. The first screen has a login box. You can enter your own name in order to try out the software yourself, or your students each fill in their name and press OK.

The next screen asks you to create a profile for the person who logged in. The screen shown here is creating a profile for Steve Martin. Once Steve clicks on the 'create' button, his profile is automatically ready for him to fill in.

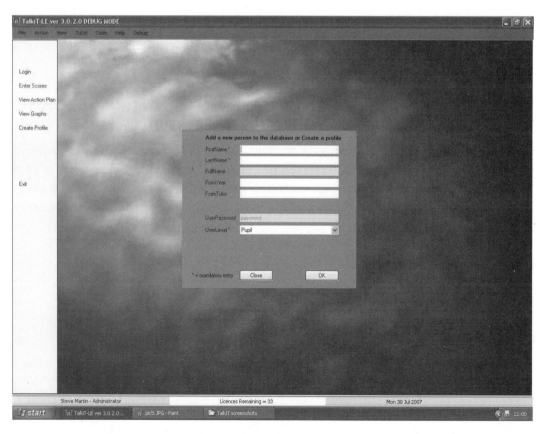

The next step is for Steve to select the 'enter scores' button on the left hand side of the screen and click on it.

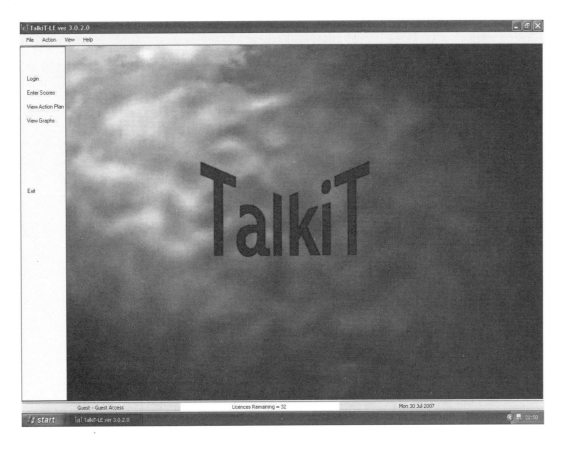

The screen shown below automatically appears and he selects his name from the drop down menu at the top of the screen.

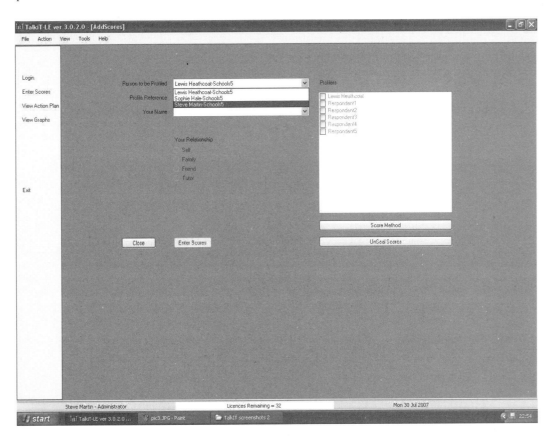

As soon as Steve clicks on his name, his name appears in the box called Person to be Profiled.

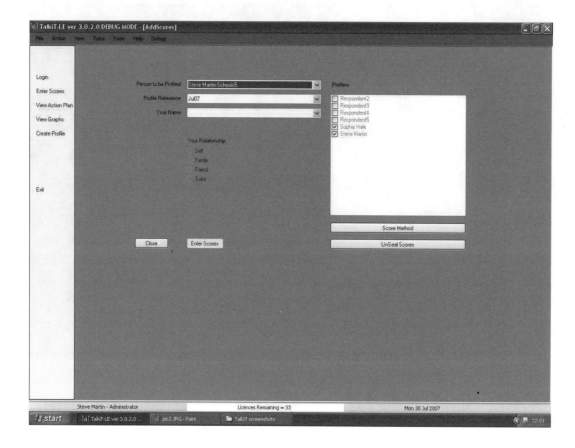

Before Steve can enter his scores he has to select his name again from the box labelled 'Your Name'. Since Steve is filling in the questionnaire for himself, the computer programme recognises this to be a 'Self' profile and the 'Enter Scores' button becomes active.

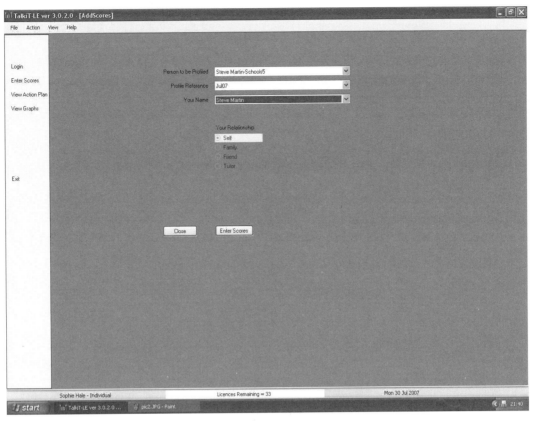

Clicking on 'Enter Scores' brings up the first question in the questionnaire and Steve can begin to enter his scores. There are audio files which will automatically run and read each question to the students as long as the computer has speakers that are switched on. In a full computer suite, you may want some students to use headphones or, if they are competent readers and don't need the audio function, there is a mute' button which they can select.

Scoring

TalkiT is a self-assessment questionnaire. Students respond to the statements by giving themselves a score from one to four where:

▶ one means 'This is not at all like me. This does not describe something that I do.'

▶ two means 'This is only a little bit like me. There are some occasions when I might behave like this, but more frequently I do not do this.'

▶ three means 'This is sometimes like me. 'I would sometimes behave in this way, but there are occasions when I would not behave this way.'

▶ four means 'This is a lot like me. On the majority of occasions this would be the way I would behave.'

The students very quickly get the hang of filling in the scores, perhaps because the format is very familiar from other contexts such as magazine quizzes. The other interesting feature of this kind of format is that students are invariably honest about themselves. Apart from a very few, they are keen to fill in the responses to the questions, eager to see the profile and get a picture of themselves. In fact they can be so honest that they recognise themselves in the graph that emerges, even if they are not that impressed with the picture that it gives back to them. One memorable occasion was when an 11 year old student saw the printout of her profile and said, 'How come you know all about me?' The graph was such an accurate representation of her that it was completely familiar, yet she did not seem to make the link between the scores she gave herself when filling in the questionnaire and the graph she received as a result.

Perhaps the most important part of filling in the questionnaire is explaining it well before the students begin. They need to understand that this is not a test. There are no right answers and no wrong answers.

The idea is to be as honest as possible about how you see yourself at this point in your life and to remember that the picture can change as you grow and develop.

Once the questionnaire has been completed, the student clicks on the 'Finish and Save' button and the programme automatically stores the profile and produces the results in the form of graphs which the student can view on screen or print.

The Questionnaire

The research that I carried out into the student's framework on what it means to do well at school revealed 12 areas of awareness from which they constructed their framework of school success. The areas of awareness are called constructs and they form the building blocks to constructing a successful life in.the world of school. The students grouped the 12 constructs into clusters or domains which mark out the territory of school success from a student's point of view.

The diagram shows the five domains and their associated 12 constructs

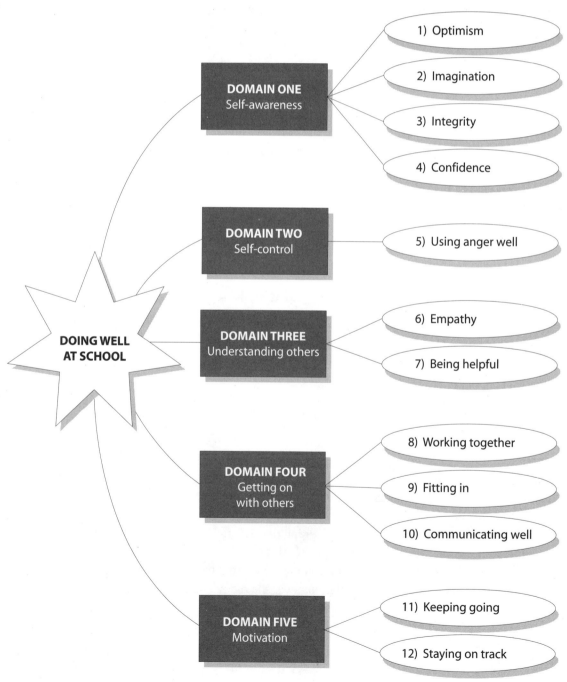

Having discovered the ways in which students construed doing well at school, I was interested in how to use this information to provide a way of working with the students so that they could get the very best out of their time at school. I therefore took all the information the students had provided and turned it into statements in a questionnaire. The resulting questionnaire has 83 statements which all relate to aspects of personal, social and emotional development as they apply in school. Students fill in their responses to the statements using the score described. Once the questionnaire is completed, the computer programme instantly generates a profile by averaging the scores in each construct. The student can select the 'View graphs' option as soon as they have completed the questionnaire and can view the feedback as either a bar graph (Gantt chart) or as a polar plot.

When the student looks at the profile, it acts like a kind of personal mirror which, when held up to them, reflects how well they think they are doing in school right now. The profile highlights areas of strength which can be used to increase success and areas of weakness that need to be looked at and developed.

Assessment for personal and social development

The TalkiT questionnaire is a way of assessing a student against the 12 constructs. It gives a picture of how the student thinks they are doing in relation to the various areas that make up personal, social and emotional competence at the time when they filled in the questionnaire. There are many arguments for and against assessing someone's emotional literacy however and it is important that we look at what assessment means in this particular context.

The aim of assessment in this context is not about giving someone a grade or level. It would be very sad if at the end of the school year, not only did Sarah have a very low level for maths and English, but she had a poor score in emotional literacy as well! Crucially, the information generated by TalkiT is for the purpose of promoting personal and social development and learning. The aim in using TalkiT to assess aspects of a student's emotional literacy is to provide accurate feedback which in itself raises self-awareness and creates interest for future learning. This is very much assessment for learning and not assessment of learning.

TalkiT profiles

The profile can be viewed as a bar graph or as a polar plot.

Bar graphs (Gannt charts)

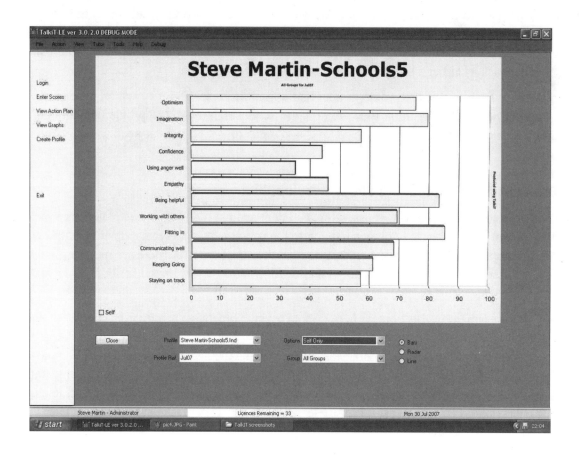

The bar graph is read like any conventional graph of this kind. The bars represent an average of the student's scores for the statements that relate to each construct and are plotted as a percentage. There is a bar for each construct and each is labelled with the name of the construct to which it refers. A longer bar represents a higher average score for a construct and a shorter bar represents a lower average score.

Polar plots

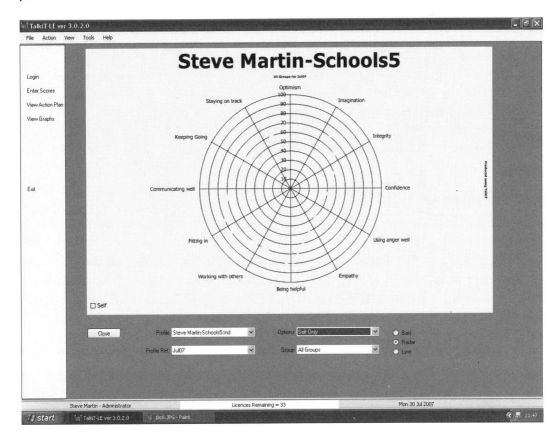

The polar plot can be seen as a wheel. It has lines that go round the hub to represent the percentage lines from 0% at the centre to 100% on the outside rim. The spokes represent the constructs. When a student fills in the questionnaire, the average scores are percentaged and the percentages are plotted on the spokes of the wheel. When a plot falls nearer the outer edge of the graph, it represents a higher average score. Plots nearer the centre represent a lower average score.

Once they understand how to use it, the students tend to prefer the polar plot. They say that bar graphs feel more competitive because they are concerned that the bars are not long enough or that they are longer or shorter than on their friend's graph. The polar plot, on the other hand, feels like a more holistic picture and it does not give rise to anxiety about whether their scores are greater than or less than someone else in the group.

It is rare for a student to have a graph which shows every point on the outer rim and it is similarly rare for all the points to be near the centre. The graph shown in the diagram is more common, with some higher scores and some lower ones. This means that almost every student has some strength and some areas for growth and development. Some students are more generous with their scoring than others, so some plots are closer in to the centre of the graph and others are nearer the outer edge, but the pattern of higher and lower scores is what you draw the student's attention to. I have been amazed and delighted throughout the development of TalkiT to discover that the picture students receive of themselves seems to feel holistic and presents an accurate reflection of how they perceive themselves. Many students say things such as, 'That's just like me,' or, 'How did it know me so well?'

Working with TalkiT profiles

When a student has filled in a TalkiT questionnaire they can view the feedback on screen. As with magazine quizzes and other self-assessment tools, this generates a high level of interest and students are very keen to find out what the feedback looks like. The danger is that, having completed the questionnaire and seen the graph, they dismiss TalkiT as 'done'. For the teacher, the skill is keeping the information alive long enough to do the developmental work that will produce growth and learning.

The first thing is to print off the graphs. When a student has a hard copy of their profile and it is placed on the table for discussion either with an adult or a peer, it takes on a greater power than when it is on screen. Even though the profiles are produced by averaging the responses that students gave to themselves, the printed graph takes on an objectivity that is very helpful to personalised discussion.

Before TalkiT profiles can be looked at and discussed in class, however, there has to be a good measure of emotional safety in the group. Section Two of this book looked at the principles that underpin working with young people for their personal and social development. At the very least, teachers find it helpful to agree groundrules with the students about how they will work together when exploring personal, social and emotional issues. It is important, for instance, that putdowns are forbidden and actively challenged if they happen.

The role of 360° assessment

One of the more unusual features of TalkiT- LE is the possibility of seeing yourself as others see you. The 360° facility in TalkiT-LE allows different people to profile each other. This facility for a friend or friends, a teacher or other adults to fill in a student's profile allows them to compare the way they see themselves with the way other people see them. Whether the perceptions agree or differ, this is a really powerful feedback tool and leads to considerable discussion. Getting positive, constructive feedback and acting on it is one of the most effective ways to improve the way we do things.

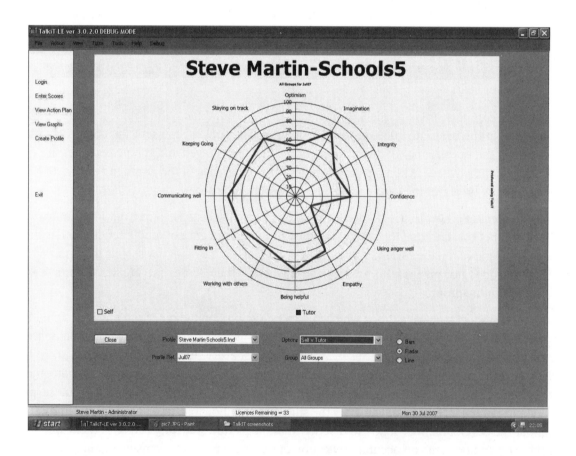

The lines on the graph are plotted in different colours to represent different people's scores. For instance, if the student has filled in a self-assessment questionnaire, the points are joined up by a yellow line. If a friend scored the questionnaire for the student, the line is red and it is shown on top of the student's own score. Similarly, family members and teachers can fill in the questionnaire about a student and the lines are plotted in different colours one on top of the other. If several friends fill in the questionnaire for an individual, their results are averaged and an average plot is shown on the graph.

Sally filled in the questionnaire for herself and then asked Natasha to fill it in for her. She was eager to see the results. The finished profiles showed that in five of the twelve constructs, the plots of Natasha's graph lay very close to Sally's. The two girls were very excited. They discussed the similarities in their scoring. Sally was heard to say, 'I am fairly confident aren't I?' and Natasha's reply, 'Yes. You are really OK with yourself.' Then they looked at the places where the two graphs did not agree. Here the discussion centred on the differences in perception. 'I don't think I get that angry.' 'But last week you had a real fall out with Vicky and shouted at her. Don't you remember?' 'Oh yeah, so I did'.

In the example cited here, the two girls were very supportive of one another. They gave and received feedback. Natasha did not use the situation to be unkind to Sally. She was encouraging with the positive feedback and gave the more difficult feedback in a very matter of fact, non-judgemental way. Sally went away to think about how well she used her anger and, in this case, asked the teacher if there were any classes she could do so that she could get better at anger management. It is likely that when students fill in the questionnaire for one another, they will be sensitive to the feedback they are giving, particularly if the same person is also filling in a questionnaire for them! Teachers and other adults using the 360° facility are best advised to highlight the potential for hurt and the need to be sensitive to the other person's feelings. It might help to have a brief session on how to give and receive feedback before doing a 360° questionnaire. The person giving the feedback has to present it honestly, sensitively and non-judgementally. They agree to focus on the positive feedback of strengths first, then to look at the more difficult aspects of the feedback. Every piece of negative feedback should be accompanied by an actual example from recent experiences so that it does not become a global description of the other person. The person receiving the feedback has to agree to remain non-defensive. They agree to accept the positive feedback without brushing it off or dismissing it. They also agree to explore the actual examples of negative feedback and rather than making excuses and think of ways in which they could do it differently next time. As both the students in the discussion have a TalkiT profile which shows self-assessment and the other person's assessment, they have a vested interest in giving feedback as carefully as they would want to receive it when it is their turn.

When a student is particularly vulnerable or on the school's special needs register, it can be very useful to ask one or two teachers to fill in a profile on the child and, if possible, to get a parent to come in to complete a questionnaire. This provides a rich source of data for any pastoral support plan (PSP) meeting, especially if the adults and the child can provide actual examples of times when strengths and weaknesses were in evidence.

The 360° feedback is a very useful way of providing feedback to an individual which can be incisive, accurate and challenging without having to become personal. There is something very helpful about being able to put the graph on the table in front of the student and talk about it almost as if it was someone else. The illusion of objectivity seems to facilitate a more open discussion about behaviour, events and possible ways of changing and growing.

Issues of confidentiality

The information provided by TalkiT LE is obviously potentially very sensitive. Sometimes students don't like what they see in their profile. One 11-year old girl shed a few tears over her profile because it showed a lower score in imagination than she thought represented her 'reality'. Imagination was a core value for this girl and to receive feedback that suggested she was less than highly imaginative was very difficult to accept. Yet a discussion that included her understanding of 'imagination' and how she used it in being able to do better at school reassured her. She saw that imagination for her involved writing imaginative stories and creating a fictitious world. She was, in fact, not very good at using imagination and creativity to help her solve problems, resolve conflicts or do better in school and was often in difficulties with both her peers and teachers. We talked about how she could use her creativity to improve her ability to do well in lessons and she set herself some targets for the following week. What started off as a difficult, sensitive and potentially demotivating feedback quickly turned into fuel that was helpful, informative and growth-producing.

In the case cited here, the girl did not want her profile to be seen by other people in the class until she had taken the time to understand it herself. The feedback in the profile had a negative effect on her self-esteem and she sought to protect her area of vulnerability until she had explained the feedback to herself. She was then happy to share the information and her learning with other members of the class group. Other students did not seem to experience this level of sensitivity. They were happy to share their profiles straight away, perhaps because their self-esteem was high enough to cope with any negative information the profile contained.

As with all types of assessment in school, the profiles are available for the teacher to see either on the computer screen or as printouts. Best practice in handling this kind of sensitive information involves negotiating who will see the feedback and how it will be used. It is important that the students view it as 'work in progress' rather than a final analysis of their social and emotional competence. The profiles are best explained as tools to help students to understand themselves better and to get a glimpse of how other people see them. They provide specific information that can be used to set personal goals and targets that will enable the individual to do well and enjoy school better. I have only ever had two students who totally refused to fill the questionnaire in. Both were boys who, for various reasons, were finding school difficult. One regretted his decision once he saw the way in which his peers dealt with the feedback. He then wanted to opportunity to fill in his questionnaire and to see what his feedback looked like. The other still wanted nothing to do with the questionnaire no matter how much other people were engaging with the feedback. This was a student whose self-esteem was very low, who became excessively angry very fast and who was struggling with most aspects of his education including basic literacy and numeracy. In his case, we talked about the questionnaire and decided together that this was probably not the best time for him to profile himself. We agreed to leave it for a few months and then review the situation, perhaps completing the questionnaire in a safer environment such as with his educational support teachers.

Action plans

TalkiT-LE has a facility that allows students to create an action plan. If they click on the 'Action Plan' button, a screen comes up giving the average scores for each construct in rank order as show in the screen print overleaf. In this example, the self scores are given in order from the largest score at the top of the page to the smallest score at the bottom. If the student prefers, he can look at the tutor's scores or his friend's scoring of them in rank order and use these scores to compare with his own. The action plan screen provides a brief definition of each construct when the cursor is held over the title, making it easy for the students to understand their scores and begin to write an action plan. There is space in the programme for notes on how well the student thinks he is doing in each construct and what they are going to do in the future to improve their performance. This action plan can be regularly visited throughout the year and, if a target is achieved, the date can be logged in the far right-hand column.

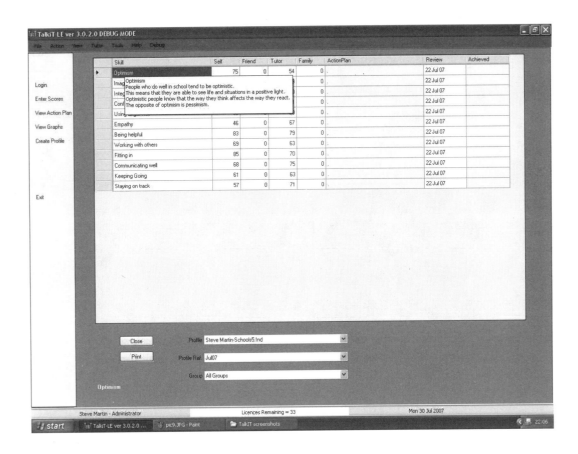

Full version TalkiT software

The full version of TalkiT has all the functions of TalkiT-LE, and several more. It is usually set up so that student profiles are created in bulk, which enables it to be used for several tutor groups, a whole year group or even a whole school. The student data is imported into the software as comma separated variable (CSV) files and once the database is established in the master TalkiT directory, individual students can log on and profile themselves in the same way as in TalkiT-LE. The individual profiles are the same as is the 360° facility. The major difference is the ability to create whole class or group profiles and to see the progress that a student makes over time by comparing the results from one time with those of a re-test at a later date.

Class or group profiles

The full version of TalkiT allows a teacher to create a group plot once a whole class or several members of a group have filled in the questionnaire. The group plot shows the group's combined responses to the questionnaire and is a representation of their corporate skill in relation to the different constructs. It is possible to view the group graph either as a single line that shows the average of the group's scores, or as individual graphs one on top of the other. The Castledown case study in Section Six explains how the teacher began his exploration of TalkiT profiles by gaining understanding of the constructs through the group profile. Looking at the group as a whole is considerably less sensitive than looking at individual profiles. Once the students understood the constructs, had grasped how the polar plot was read, and made an estimation of the group's performance in each construct, the estimate was compared to the actual computer plot. The differences between the estimate and the actual plot provided a rich source of discussion about both group behaviour and individual contributions to the whole. This activity led naturally on to an examination of the individual profiles.

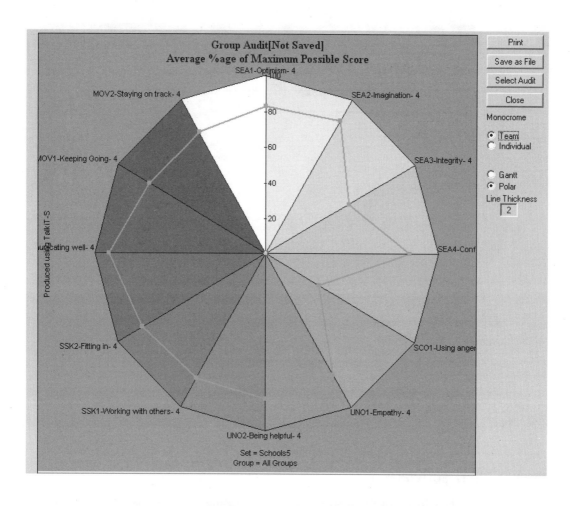

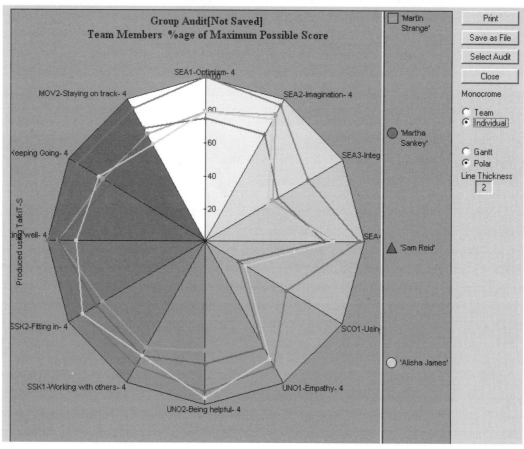

Alongside a combined group profile, teachers can see how individual members of the group contribute to the overall score in any construct. It is likely that they will not share this information with the group unless there is a good measure of emotional security and supportive behaviour. On the other hand, the comparison between plots helps the teacher to decide which students could help one another in developing different areas of emotional literacy.

The students can be paired or grouped to include some that are strong in relation to a particular construct and some that are weaker. Exchanging stories and examples of real-life events, writing storyboards or creating role plays helps all the students in the group to grow and develop in their skills.

Changes over time

Another additional function found in TalkiT that is not present in TalkiT-LE is the ability to take the test again after a period of time and then compare the scores given on the first occasion with those given on subsequent occasions. This facility helps a student to see how much progress they are making, which areas still need work and any areas in which they think they were better last year than they are in the current year. It is important to note that scores sometimes drop rather than rise in the short-term. This is because increased self-awareness can cause a person to score themselves more realistically or more harshly than they did when they were unable to observe their own behaviour. Over time, this increase in self-awareness will enable the student to take action and the higher scores will eventually follow successful personal interventions.

Summary

In this section you have:

► learned how to use the TalkiT-LE software accompanying this book

► thought about the use of questionnaires and profiles as a way of promoting self-awareness and personal and social development

► considered the issues of confidentiality and sensitivty in this kind of work

► heard about a fuller version of Talk-iT that might be of use in your school.

Section Six

TalkiT Case Studies

Mayfield Middle School (Isle of Wight)

I used TalkiT with My Year 8 classes and it generated a huge amount of interest, discussion and indeed fun. I feel that I have only just begun to scratch the surface with regards to the potential 'power' of this tool.

I had prepared the ground prior to the questionnaire by booking the school hall. We imagined a line or scale which I labelled with each of the constructs in turn. One end of the imaginary line was 'like me' and the other end 'not like me'. This enabled the students to place themselves where they thought they fell with regard to particular constructs and we were able to discuss what we all understood by the vocabulary used in the constructs. When the students had placed themselves on a line for a particular construct, I asked for feedback on why they were at a particular point. Rather than get feedback from the whole class I decided to ask for individual responses. They were surprisingly honest. They volunteered quite willingly their thoughts on why they saw themselves in a particular place.

I find in PSHE that there is always the problem that some people respond the same as their friends because they are 'following the group'. In this work, however, individuals thought autonomously though it wouldn't have mattered if they had copied one another. At the end of the day it was the discussion about their understanding and perceptions that was important at this stage of the process, not their honesty.

The next lesson we filled in the questionnaires and because I had explained what the outcome would be – a profile – they were all very keen to view their results. Very few of them expressed total surprise and I did manage to get round all of them to summarise what it showed. What did prove particularly successful was paired work next lesson when they completed the questionnaires for their close friends. One couple actually shrieked with pleasure when they discovered that their profiles were almost identical. It made them feel particularly good that they were able to 'read' their friend so accurately!

Others had long discussions where discrepancies occurred – I just wished I had had a tape recorder to catch all their conversations.

Where I needed more time was to act on the results. I would like to do much more work to improve social and emotional growth and learning. Trying to deliver the PSHE and now statutory Citizenship curriculum in one lesson per week presents a huge dilemma in how to best use the time.

Our Special Needs Co-ordinator (SENCO) is also very interested in the tool because she noticed some very interesting results for some of the pupils she works with and has asked me to do some work with her to explore how we can best use this information – and where we go from here.

(Head of PSHE)

The George Ward School, Melksham

I used TalkiT with a Year 7 tutor group that was having particular difficulties gelling as a group. The class was taught as a tutor group for Humanities, English, PSHE, design and technology and languages. The specific difficulties within this group made them very unpredictable. They had an excellent and experienced tutor with whom they were calm and controlled. In other areas of the school, there seemed to be no way to predict how they would behave. Sometimes staff found them delightful to teach, interested, lively, imaginative and cooperative. At other times they were impossible to teach because of noisy aggression, lack of self-control and an inability to accommodate or listen to each other.

The group had taken part in a more than a term of Circle Time activities during PSHE before they filled in their TalkiT profiles. In PSHE lessons they had considered friendship issues, working together, giving and receiving feedback and developing confidence. Despite the work they had done, the response to the questionnaire was mixed. Most students were very keen to fill it in. They were very honest with and about themselves and eager to see the resulting profile. Two boys (close friends) in the group found it very difficult to fill in the questionnaire. They were reluctant to disclose anything about themselves. In the end they both spoiled their questionnaires by not answering questions or scoring 0.

Another two students (one boy and one girl) were suspicious of TalkiT and wanted to know what it was for and who would see it. Only when they were assured that the resulting profile was theirs and they could show it to people or not as they chose, were they comfortable enough to complete the questionnaire. They both successfully completed the questionnaire and were very happy with the results, confidently sharing them with their neighbours.

Filling in the responses to the questionnaire did not present any problem to the students. They understood the questions and the scoring scheme. It took them an average of 20 minutes and then they wanted to see the profiles, which were instantly available on screen. Looking at the profiles created a lot of discussion about comparative scores, strengths and weaknesses. Once the students had filled in their questionnaires and looked at the profiles on screen, I printed them off so that the tutor and I could use them in tutorial time.

At the next tutorial session, each student was given their printed profile and a student booklet that explained each of the constructs. They were then asked to work alone to identify their three strongest constructs and then look up what they meant. A member of support staff had agreed to work with me to enable even the poorest readers and those who were likely to be baffled by the graph to access the information. Once they clearly understood what the profile was telling them about themselves, they were put into groups of students with similar strengths. In their groups, they talked about actual examples from their lives to illustrate their strongest constructs.

They were reminded of the groundrules for giving and receiving feedback from one another so that a respectful space was assured. They were also given the option of not sharing their profile, but of joining the appropriate group to listen and not share. In the event only the two students did not take part in the discussion groups. One of the boys who had been unwilling to fill in his opted out entirely and we agreed that he could read a book during the tutorial lesson. The other student who had difficulty taking part was a girl who looked at her profile and gradually became more and more silent. When I noticed how withdrawn she had become, I went to sit next to her. It turned out that she was upset because the profile did not show her to be as good at fitting in as she thought she was. She was a child who placed very high value on being part of a group. When we talked about what fitting in meant in the TalkiT questionnaire, she was able to look at her own life and see why she wasn't as skilled as she had thought. She was someone who tended to give in all the time to other people in order to fit in. Her own sense of integrity was often compromised in the process. She felt much better by the end of the lesson and left feeling happy with the feedback she had received. The other boy who did not fill in his questionnaire chose to take part in a discussion group and at the end of the lesson was reassured enough about the feedback to want to do the questionnaire in his next PSHE lesson.

The discussion was very focussed. Students were interested and involved, comfortable to share some very personal information even with people that they often fell out with in normal lesson time. It created connections across the tutor group and a level of self-disclosure that had not been typical of other PSHE lessons.

Once they had talked about their strengths, the groups were re-convened around the areas of greatest weakness. Once again the students told stories from their experiences. They told of times when they had not kept to the school rules, when they had been angry, when they had not fitted in or been less confident than they would have liked. Still there was a much greater level of self-disclosure than ever before. The knock on effect of the TalkiT discussions was the foundation for a much better understanding of one another in the group.

The group audit for the class gave the tutor and PSHE teacher a much clearer picture of the overall strengths and weaknesses in the group. This information allowed them to plan some specific remedial work to address areas of strength. It also provided actual data to use for encouraging students and boosting their self-esteem, or to draw on when talking to parents.

(PSHE teacher)

Castledown School, Wiltshire

We used TalkiT with a full cohort of year 7 pupils. In the year 7 classes, before we did the TalkiT questionnaire, we had a PSHE Circle Time lesson where we explored each of the constructs so that the pupils developed a vocabulary around the five groups and 12 constructs. Before the circle, I made 12 cards with a construct written on each and the page number in the student booklet where they could find the definition. I also made a large polar plot identical to the one found in the TalkiT software on sugar paper for the middle of the circle.

The 26 students in the circle were put into pairs (with two threes) and each pair was given a piece of card with a construct printed on it alongside a booklet that explained each construct. The pupils had only the vaguest idea of what 'integrity' and 'optimism' meant before they looked at the appropriate page in the booklet, but they soon understood. Once a pair had found out what their construct meant, they had to think of an actual example when they had seen someone or a group of people in the class using the construct.

After five minutes or so, each pair had discussed what the construct meant and had thought of an example. We then went round the circle and each pair in turn held up their card and explained the construct to the rest of the group. They then plotted how well they thought the class as a whole did on that construct on the big polar graph in the middle of the circle. One by one the 12 pairs (groups) gave a definition of their construct and plotted how well they thought the group did across all their subject areas. As they plotted the group score, the pair had to provide at least one piece of evidence from the last week to substantiate their estimate. No one else in the group was allowed to argue with the pair's estimation of the group's performance. After all 12 constructs had been explained, the plotted points were joined up on the graph in the middle of the circle. Students were then invited to make comments about different plots and provide evidence to either support it or challenge it.

By the end of the lesson, the students had a good understanding of the 12 constructs, they had developed a vocabulary that formed the foundation for work on emotional literacy and they had thought about their performance as a group. They were told that once they had filled in their individual TalkiT questionnaires, a group plot would be produced and then they could compare it with the one they had estimated this lesson.

The introductory lesson made an excellent platform for filling in the questionnaire and for understanding the individual feedback that each student received. They knew how to read the graph, what each construct meant and they had some idea of real examples to provide evidence of the constructs.

Using the TalkiT profiles, we then worked on developing some of our weaker skills. We did some work on anger management and on confidence building. The students were particularly interested in optimism and how to be more optimistic in the light of receiving negative feedback in lessons like Maths and

English. We used drama techniques such as role play and cooperative games to develop confidence, empathy and optimism. There is much more that we could do with TalkiT and we hope to use it in future years. We envisage a real use in helping teachers to understand how a group functions (or fails to function) and would like to explore sharing the group results with subject staff for a particular tutor group. This would give the subject teacher insights into the group without breaching the confidentiality of the individual.

(PSHE teacher and tutor)

Section Seven

Student Handbook and Resources

The student handbook

The student handboook contains sections on the five Domains, the twelve constructs and the TalkIT program. The booklet was originally researched and written with young people between the ages of 11-14. The handbook could be used to introduce the classroom activities in Section Four, the Talk IT program in Section Five or in any other way that best meets the needs of the students.

The student handbook as well as the student activity sheets are on the accompanying CD-ROM.

Useful resources for promoting emotional literacy work in school

If you have enjoyed this book, if you have found any resonance with your own experience in reaching young people and motivating them to greater engagement with school, then there is more.

The CD-ROM that accompanies this book is TalkiT-LE, a short version of the TalkiT programme. It provides you with 30 profiles, enough to use with a class of young people so that you can get to grips with the ideas and try them out.

If you are interested in finding out about the full version of TalkiT, please visit www.marilytew.co.uk or office@marilyntew.co.uk

It is not possible to cite all the excellent resources that are available to support a school's work in relation to emotional literacy. Here I present some of the resources that I have found to be both useful and information in this area of work.

Antidote (2003) *The Emotional Literacy Handbook*: **Promoting whole-school strategies. London: Fulton.**

This book provides a clear exposition of emotional literacy and why it matters to schools. It explores ways in which schools have provided contexts and strategies for increasing emotionally literate ways of being and behaving in school for both adults and children.

Bowkett, S. (1999) *Self-Intelligence: A handbook for Developing Confidence, Self-Esteem and Interpersonal Skills.* **Stafford: Network Educational Press.**

This is an activities book to use with children and young people. Every page provides ideas and worksheets to develop sensory acuity, enhance emotional literacy, encourage a creative attitude and promote the use of relaxation techniques.

Cowling, A. & Vine, P. (2001) *Bridging the Circle: Transition through Quality Circle Time.* **Trowbridge: Positive Press.**

A set of 12 lessons specifically aimed at the transition. Six lessons are taught in Year 6 before the children move to secondary school and six lessons are for Year 7 after the transition. Each lesson is designed as a Circle Time session. Photocopiable resources and lesson plans are provided.

Corrie, C. (2003) *Becoming Emotionally Intelligent.* **Stafford: Network Educational Press.**

This is a book packed full of wisdom, case studies and activities for developing emotional intelligence in children while becoming more aware of your own.

Dewar, R., Palser, K. and Notley, M. (1989) *Games Games Games II.* **London: The Woodcraft Folk.**

Games Games Games II and *Games Games Games III* are both excellent sources of games and activities for using as starters in PSHE lessons, tutorials and Circle Time sessions for introducing topics related to emotional literacy.

Faupel, A., Herrick, E., and Sharp, P. (1998) *Anger Management: A Practical Guide.* **London: Fulton.**

As it says, this a practical guide for adults working with anger management. It includes a good summary of the theory of anger and some practical activities and worksheets to use with young people.

Fuller, A., Bellhouse, B., & Johnson, G. (2002) *The Heart Masters for school children aged 12 to 14.* **Bristol: Lucky Duck.**

This is an excellent source of additional worksheets and activities to use with students in the early years of secondary school.

Mosely, J. and Tew, M. (1998) *Quality Circle Time for the Secondary School: A handbook of good practice.* **London: Fulton.**

Quality Circle Time had largely been viewed as a primary school approach until this publication, which explores the application of a whole school approach to listening systems in secondary schools.

Schilling, D. (1997) *50 Activities for Teaching Emotional Intelligence.* **Level II: Middle School. US: Jalmar Press Inc.**

Schilling, D. (1999) *50 Activities for teaching emotional intelligence.* **Level III: High School. US: Jalmar Press Inc.**

Both these resources provide ideas and activities for using with pre-teens and teenaged young people to develop their emotional intelligence.

Stanford, G., and Stoate, P. (1990) *Developing Effective Classroom Groups.* **Chippenham: Acora Books.**

This is a resource for those who want to build better learning communities in their class groups. It explains the theory of group formation and functioning with many ideas of practical activities to use with young people to build effective groups.

Tew, M., Read, M. and Potter, H. (2006) *Circles, PSHE and Citizenship: The value of Circle Time in secondary schools.* **Bristol: Lucky Duck Books.**

Based on a case study, this book explores the use of Circle Time for all aspects of the PSHE and Citizenship curriculum, including developing the skills, attitudes and values of emotional literacy. The practical experiences of five years of researching the process of introducing Circle Time into a secondary school identifies the strengths, weaknesses and difficulties of implementing and embedding change. The main theme of the book is to encourage and provide confidence to those teachers who want to use

Circle Time as a vehicle for engaging young people in their own personal and social learning so that they change and develop as a result.

Weare, K. (2000) *Promoting Mental, Emotional and Social Health: A whole school approach.* **London: Routledge.**

As the title says, this book examines the factors that need to be taken into account when developing a whole school approach to social and emotional health and well-being. It provides definitions of the many terms used in the field of mental, emotional and social health, helping the reader to make sense of the field of knowledge. It goes on to explain the principles that underpin adopting a whole school approach to support this work.

Weare, K. (2004) *Developing the Emotionally Literate School.* **London: Sage Publications.**

Once a school has committed to a whole school approach to emotional literacy, the senior team would find this book a useful guide to the scope of the work and the support that is available.

Useful web-based resources

CASEL (The Collaborative for Academic Social and Emotional Learning)
www.casel.org

Centre for Social and Emotional Education (CSEE)
www.csee.net

Committee for Children
www.cfchildren.org

Emotional Health and Well-being Support for Young People
www.lifebytes.gov.uk

Emotional Literacy Advocates
www.nwlink.com

EQ Network Europe
www.equeurope.6seconds.org

The National Emotional Literacy Interest Group
www.nelig.com

Pupiline
www.pupiline.net

Six Seconds
www.6seconds.org

Teachernet
www.teachernet.gov.uk/pshe

Transforming Conflict
www.transformconflict.org

Transforming Schools
www.transformingschools.org.uk

Bibliography and References

Antidote (2003) *The Emotional Literacy Handbook: Promoting whole-school strategies.* London: Fulton.

Ballard, J. (1982) *Circlebook: A leader handbook for conducting Circle Time, a curriculum of affect.* New York, Irvington Publishers.

Bliss, T., Robinson, G., & Maines, B. (1995) *Developing Circle Time: Takes Circle Time Much Further.* Bristol: Lucky Duck Publishing.

Bliss, T., & Tetley, J. (1993) *Circle Time: For infant, junior and secondary schools.* Bristol: Lucky Duck Publishing.

Bliss, T. & Robinson, G. (1993) *Coming Round to Circle Time.* Bristol: Lucky Duck Publishing.

Bohensky, A. (2001) *Anger Management Workbook for Kids and Teens.* Growth Pub.

Brandes, D. and Ginnis, P. (1986) *A Guide to Student-Centred Learning.* Oxford: Basil Blackwell.

Button, L. (1971) *Discovery and Experience.* London: Oxford University Press.

Button, L. (1982) *Group Tutoring for the Form Teacher.* London: Hodder and Stoughton.

Bowkett, S. (1999) *Self-Intelligence: A handbook for Developing Confidence, Self-Esteem and Interpersonal Skills.* Stafford: Network Educational Press.

Collins (2004) *Essential Dictionary & Thesaurus.* Glasgow: HarperCollins.

Corrie, C. (2003) *Becoming Emotionally Intelligent.* Stafford: Network Educational Press.

Cowling, A. & Vine, P. (2001) *Bridging the Circle: Transition through Quality Circle Time.* Trowbridge: Positive Press.

Curry, M. & Bromfield, C. (1994) *Circle Time.* Stafford: Nasen.

Deakin Crick, R., Broadfoot, P., Tew, M., Jelfs, H., Randall, E., Prosser, G., Temple, S., (2004) The *Ecology of Learning: a cross sectional exploration of relationships between learner-centred variables in five schools.* Bristol: Graduate School of Education, University of Bristol.

Deci, E. L., and Ryan, R. M. (1991) *A motivational approach to self: Integration in personality.* In R. Dienstbier (Ed.) Nebraska symposium on motivation pp 237-288. Lincoln, NE: University of Nebraska Press.

Dewar, R., Palser, K. and Notley, M. (1989) *Games Games Games II.* London: The Woodcraft Folk.

Dewey, J. (1938) *Education and Experience.* New York: Collier Macmillan.

Dwek, C. S. (1999) *Self-Theories: Their role in motivation, personality and development.* Lilllington, NC: Edwards Brothers.

Faupel, A., Herrick, E. and Sharp, P. (1998) *Anger Management: A Practical Guide.* London: Fulton.

Fitzell, S. A. (2004) *Transforming Anger to Personal Power: A Curriculum Guide for Grades 6 Through 12.* Manchester NH: Cogent Catalyst Publications.

Francis, E. (2001) *'Dialogical Inquiry' The Real Dialogue Conference Brochure*, Belfast. London: Antidote.

Fuller, A., Bellhouse, B., & Johnson, G. (2002) *The Heart Masters for school children aged 12 to 14.* Bristol: Lucky Duck.

Gardner, H. (1983) *Multiple Intelligence: The Theory in Practice.* London: Basic Books.

Gardner, H. (1991) *The Unschooled Mind: How children think and how schools should teach.* London: Fontana.

Gardner, H. (1993) *Frames of Mind: The Theory of Multiple Intelligences (second ed.)* London: Fontana Press.

Goleman, D. (1996) *Emotional Intelligence.* New York: Bantam Books.

Goleman D. (1998) *Working with Emotional Intelligence.* New York: Bantam Books.

Johnson, D. S., Johnson, R. and Anderson, D. (1983) *'Social Interdependence and Classroom Climate.'* The Journal of Psychology 114 pp 135-142.

Jones, B. F (1990) *'The New Definition of Learning: The First Step to School Reform.' Restructuring to promote learning in America's schools: A guidebook.* Elmhurst, IL: North Central Regional Educational Laboratory.

Kelly, G. A. (1955) *The Psychology of Personal Constructs.* New York: Norton.

Kohn, A. (1991) *'Caring Kids: The Role of the Schools.'* Phi Delta Kappan 72(7) pp 496-506.

Mann, A. H. (1994) *Route to Master Facilitator.* Bradford: Resource Masters of Change.

Maslow, A. (1962) *Towards a Psychology of Being.* New York: Van Nostrand Reinhold.

McKay, G. D., and Maybell, S. A. (2004) *Calming the Family Storm: Anger Management for Moms, Dads and All the Kids.* California: Impact Publishers.

Mosley, J. (1993) *Turn Your School Round.* Cambridge: LDA.

Mosley, J. (1996) *Quality Circle Time.* Cambridge: LDA.

Mosley, J., & Tew, M. (1998) *Quality Circle Time in the Secondary School: A Handbook of Good Practice.* London: Fulton.

Outhwaite, W. (1994) *Habermas: A critical introduction.* Cambridge: Polity Press.

Neill, A. S. (1962) *Summerhill.* London: Victor Gollancz Ltd.

Park, J. (2001) *'Reasons for Talking'.* The Real Dialogue Conference Brochure, Belfast. London: Antidote.

Rogers, C. (1986a) *Freedom to learn for the 80s.* Colombus, Ohio: Charles E. Merrill.

Rousseau, Salovey, P., and Mayer, J. D. (1990) Emotional intelligence. *Imagination, Cognition and Personality,* 9 185-211.

Schilling, D. (1997) *50 Activities for Teaching Emotional Intelligence.* Level 11: Middle School. Jalmar Press Inc.

Schilling, D. (1999) *50 Activities for Teaching Emotional Intelligence.* Level 111: High School. Jalmar Press Inc.

Segal, J. (1997) *Raising your Emotional Intelligence: A practical Guide.* New York: Henry Holt.

Seligman, M. (1990) *Learned Optimism: How to Change Your Mind and Your Life.* New York: Pocket Books.

Seligman, M (1996) *The optimistic child: Proven Program to Safeguard Children from Depression & Build Lifelong Resilience.* Boston, Mass: Hoghton Mifflin.

Sharp, P. (2001) *Nurturing emotional literacy: A practical guide for teachers, parents and those in the caring professions.* London: Fulton.

Slavin, R. E. (1985) *'Cooperative Learning: Applying Contact Theory in Desegregated Schools'* Journal of Social Issues 41(3) pp 45-62.

Smith, A. (1998) *Accelerated learning in practice: brain-based methods for accelerating motivation and achievement Stafford*: Network Educational Press.

Smith, C. (2003a) *Circle Time in Secondary Schools.* Bristol: Lucky Duck Publishing.

Smith, C. (2003b) *Concluding Circle Time with Secondary Students.* Bristol, Lucky Duck.

Smith, C. (2004) *Circle Time for Adolescents.* Bristol: Lucky Duck Publishing.

Stanford, G., and Stoate, P. (1990) *Developing Effective Classroom Groups.* Chippenham: Acora Books.

Steiner, C. (1997) *Achieving Emotional Literacy.* London: Bloomsbury Publishing.

Stenhouse, L. (1967) *Culture and Education.* London: Nelson.

Stenhouse, L. (1975) *An Introduction to Curriculum Research and Development.* London: Heinemann Ed. Books Ltd.

Tew, M. W. (2002) *The lifeworld of year 7 pupils: personal development and learning.* Unpublished doctoral thesis, University of Bristol.

Tew, M., Read, M. and Potter, H. (2006) *Circles, PSHE and Citizenship: The Value of Circle Time in Secondary Schools,* Bristol: Lucky Duck/ Paul Chapman Publishing.

Thorndike, E. L. (1920) *Intelligence and its uses.* Harper's Magazine, 140. 227-235.

Weare, K. (2000) *Promoting Mental, Emotional and Social Health: A whole school approach.* London: Routledge.

Weare, K. (2004) *Developing the Emotionally Literate School.* London: Sage Publications.

White, M. (1990) *Circle Time, Cambridge Journal of Education,* 20 (1) 53 – 56.

White, M. (1991) *Self-Esteem – Its Meaning and Value in Schools: How to help children learn readily and behave well.* Kansas: Daniels Publishing.

Wilde, J. (1997) *Hot Stuff to Help Kids Chill Out: The Anger Management Book.* Richmond IN: LGR Publishing.

Wilde, J. (2002) *Anger Management in Schools: Alternatives to Student Violence.* Switzerland: Technomic Publishing.